The Prisoners' Diaries

The Prisoners' Diaries
Palestinian Voices from the Israeli Gulag

Edited by Norma Hashim

"The Prisoners' Diaries" are translations of accounts dictated in Arabic by former Palestinian prisoners of the Israelis.

Early in 2013, Malaysian social activist Norma Hashim resolved to get these diaries translated and published. She gathered a like-minded team determined to do whatever they can to help raise awareness of the plight of the Palestinian prisoners.

By publishing these diaries, they are now reaching out to people of goodwill, appealing to you for help to put a stop to a saga of abuse.

Published by

Islamic Human Rights Commission

www.ihrc.org.uk

Published in Great Britain in 2013
by Islamic Human Rights Commission
PO Box 598, Wembley, HA9 7XH

Copy text edited by Mark Gibson
Design & Typeset: Red Bamboo Creative Sdn Bhd, Malaysia
Cover illustration by Foong Teck Hee http://creativetrees.blogspot.com

Distributed in the United Kingdom, Europe and North America
by Islamic Human Rights Commission

Distributed in Malaysia
by Palestine Mall
Registered trademark of Deen Reach Sdn Bhd (1001980-D)
Lot A03A-G, Plaza Jelutong Persiaran Gerbang Utama
Bukit Jelutong, 40150 Shah Alam, Malaysia.
Email: palestinemall@deenreach.com
Website: www.palestinemall.net
http://theprisonersdiaries.blogspot.com

Printed in Turkey by Mega Printing

ISBN 978-1-903718-92-6

Dedicated to
the hunger striker Samer Issawi and
all Palestinian prisoners –
past, present and future –
illegally held in Israeli jails

Drawing of Samer Issawi by Shahd Abusalama

CONTENTS

Preface

THIS is a book like no other book. It is a compilation of the writings of Palestinian prisoners who have been freed, and reflect the pain and sufferings of forgotten prisoners, of prisoners without hope, of prisoners who may never be free again, who will die incarcerated in their prison.

That this is happening in our age is hard to believe. We live in the age of freedom, the age when the already free still demand for more freedom. Yet there is no freedom at all for these prisoners of the Israelis. They can hardly move in the cells they are confined to. They can neither exercise the body and limbs nor their minds. They are total prisoners not because they are criminals but because they crave to be free like other people in a free country.

It is difficult not to feel the pain that they suffer as one reads their writings. That they are suffering like this as we enjoy our freedoms seem incongruous. Yet they are truly suffering.

If we cannot release them, then the least we can do is to tell the world about them. Maybe we will stir the conscience of the world and the world will do something for them which will make our civilisation truly civilised.

Tun Dr. Mahathir bin Mohamad
Former Prime Minister of Malaysia

Foreword

Dr. Mahmoud M. Alhirthani
CPDS Chairman

These diaries have been published while Palestinian prisoners are on hunger strike for freedom. Two of them – Samer Issawi and Ayman Sharawna – have been on hunger strike for more than seven months.

No human being would willingly endure such privation without good reason. Their resolution bears witness to the terrible fact of the Israeli occupation of Palestine, and the almost unimaginably wretched conditions in which Palestinian prisoners are held. Yet at the same time it expresses the dauntless courage and limitless dignity of the human spirit.

As at 1 January 2013, 4,743 prisoners were held in Israeli jails. Of these, 178 are still being held under "administrative detention orders" – which means without charge or trial. The longest administrative detention has so far lasted four and a half years.

The list of names of the sufferers for freedom is long.

In 2011, 1,027 Palestinians were released from Israeli captivity with psychological wounds so deep that they will never heal. Of these, only a handful were able to recollect fragments of their ordeal. 38 of them have related their experiences to Arabic-speaking journalists. 22 of these accounts have now been translated into English by two young volunteers and are published here for the first time.

It is important to recall that these pages document the experience of only a tiny fraction of the total number of Palestinian prisoners held in appalling conditions in 27 Israeli jails. 18 human souls were in solitary confinement in tomb-like cells without fresh air or sunlight – some, such as Abdellhadi Ghunaim, endured such misery for 12 years. 120 Palestinians have spent more than 20 years in Israeli jails.

For the last six years, most prisoners from the Gaza Strip have not seen their families. Yahya Sulaih's mother died waiting in front of the International Committee of the Red Cross office for the bus to take her to see her imprisoned son.

The abuse of Palestinian prisoners is not only a human tragedy but an international scandal. In publishing these diaries we are hoping to reach out to people of goodwill who can help to alleviate such terrible anguish by prayer, by raising awareness of the situation, or by advocacy.

This book has been a labour of compassion and love, and we at the Centre for Political & Development Studies (CPDS), would like to offer our heartfelt thanks to the children of the late Chief Justice Hashim Yeop Sani, and above all his daughter, Norma Hashim, for caring enough to have the diaries published in English. Without her unflinching support for the Palestinian cause, the stories that you are now reading would not have seen the light of day.

10 March 2013

Acknowledgements

My friends at Viva Palestina Malaysia first introduced me to the Palestinian cause, and their selflessness never fails to move me.

This book has been produced in close collaboration with the Centre for Political & Development Studies who was my contact with all the prisoners.

It reflects the commitment of many individuals, particularly the two translators Yousef M. Aljamal and Raed A. Qaddura, who carefully rendered the diaries into English, and Joe Catron who first edited the translated texts; and the journalists who interviewed the prisoners: Yasser Albanna, Fihaa Shalash, Haitham Ghrab, Samah Almazyan, Rasha Farahat, Khaled Krizim, Moath Alamodi, Mohammed Alminarawi, Maha Shahwan and Hanan Mteer.

The writings of journalist Ramzy Baroud, who contributed the Introduction to this book, have informed and energised me.

I feel profound respect for the efforts of Gavan Kelly and Addameer, the Prisoner Support and Human Rights Association. Doa'a Ahmed and the Ministry of Detainees' Affairs in Gaza have also been unstintingly helpful.

To all my friends in Gaza and the West Bank who inspire me with their faith and perseverance – I say, if you don't give up, I won't give up!

I also owe heartfelt thanks to Rozini Amin for her invaluable assistance in every area of this project, and to

Mark Gibson for his deft editing of the copy text and to Low Seong Chai of Red Bamboo Creative Sdn Bhd for further heightening the visual impact of the book with his graphic design.

I am forever grateful to my parents for teaching me to love the written word and to the Hashim family for supporting the Hashim Sani library project at the Centre for Political & Development Studies. I also wish to thank my children Faris, Hafiz, Adam, Danial and Nazim for putting up with my long nights spent at the computer. And finally, for his support and belief in every project I pursue, I offer my deepest gratitude to my beloved husband, Azman.

- Norma Hashim

Introduction

Ramzy Baroud

RAED Abu Hammad was found dead on the floor of his cell in an Israeli prison in April, 2010. He was ill, yet was kept in solitary confinement. The death of the 27-year-old young man inspired little media coverage. "Issa Qaraqi, minister of prisoner affairs in the Western-backed government of Palestinian President Mahmoud Abbas," reported the Israeli daily newspaper Haaretz, demanded "an investigation".[1] Israeli Prison Service authorities offered little by way of explanation. And as abruptly as the seemingly negligible news emerged, it disappeared.

Raed's death, of course, is neither the beginning nor the end of a very painful chapter of Palestinian resistance. There are thousands of Palestinian prisoners in Israeli jails, many of whom are held in solitary confinement for resisting the brutal policies of the Israeli occupation; for seeking freedom; for fighting for the honour of their families, their people. However, they remain faceless and nameless to Israeli and Western media. To the Palestinian people, they represent the finest of Palestine's fighters, a collective retort to injustice, the antithesis to the politicking of the self-serving politicians, and much more.

In a prisoner exchange that saw the release of Gilad Shalit, the only Israeli soldier held by Palestinians in Gaza, on 18 October 2011, 1,027 Palestinian prisoners were released in two phases. These freed prisoners were spared the chains of their small cells, yet found themselves confined to larger open-air prisons, divided between Gaza – under a harsh siege since 2007 – and the West Bank and East Jerusalem, sliced by the ever-growing Apartheid Wall and dotted with hundreds of military checkpoints. It was a bittersweet moment, as these men and women emerged from their buses, to be greeted by their families and thousands of cheering Palestinians, only to resume another long-term sentence, behind a wall, or at the other side of a military checkpoint.

While some of these released prisoners were, once again, unlawfully apprehended by the Israeli army, perhaps to return to the very cells in which they lived for many months or years, others carried on with life as best as they could.

Hana Shalabi was one of those freed prisoners. Her story is troublingly typical. She has spent 25 months under what Israel calls 'administrative detention," a bizarre legal system that allows Israel to hold Palestinian political activists indefinitely and without charge or trial. She was released in October 2011 as part of the prisoner exchange deal, only to be kidnapped by soldiers a few months later. "She was beaten, blindfolded and forcibly strip-searched and assaulted by a male Israeli soldier," the Palestinian Council of Human Rights Organizations said.[2]

With no international action to oblige Israel to accept that "No one shall be subjected to arbitrary arrest, detention or exile," – as stated in Article 9, Universal Declaration of Human Rights – Hana had little choice but to follow the path of other political prisoners. On 16

February 2012, she went on hunger strike. 43 days later, Hana was deported to Gaza, and was only allowed to be united with her family, under Israeli military supervision, for a tear-filled 20 minutes at the Erez crossing. It will be another three years before they see her again.[3]

Hana's hunger strike followed that of Khader Adnan, who, at the time, had staged the longest hunger strike ever carried out by a Palestinian prisoner. Khader endured for 66 days to send a message to his jailer that life without dignity is not worth living.

Neither Hana's case, nor that of Khader is isolated by any means. Charlotte Kates, who is active with The National Lawyers Guild wrote, "Imprisonment is a fact of life for Palestinians; over 40% of Palestinian men in the West Bank have spent time in Israeli detention or prisons. There are no Palestinian families that have not been touched by the scourge of mass imprisonment as a mechanism of suppression."[4]

According to Addameer Prisoner Support & Human Rights Association [5], "Since the beginning of the Israeli occupation of Palestinian territories in 1967, over 800,000 Palestinians have been detained by Israel. This forms approximately 20% of the total Palestinian population in the Occupied Palestinian Territories (OPT)."[6]

Samer Issawi, was one of those released in the prisoners exchange deal. However, a few months later he was arrested by Israeli forces for supposedly violating the conditions of his release. Issawi's response was staging a hunger strike and on 31 March 2013 he completed 253 days of his hunger strike in protest of his unlawful detention by Israel.

Still, that was hardly a unique phenomenon. Issawi is one of seven brothers, six of whom spent time in Israeli prisons for their political beliefs. One of the brothers, Fadi, was killed by Israeli soldiers in 1994, a few days after celebrating his 16th birthday. Even their sister, Sherine, was arrested by Israeli soldiers during a hearing concerning her brother Samer on 18 December 2012.

On that day, "Samer was publicly beaten in the Jerusalem Magistrates Court after he tried to greet his family," reported The Palestine Monitor. "He was dragged from his wheelchair and carried away, repeatedly crying out as he was hit on his chest by the guards around him." In fact, the Issawi family and the entire neighbourhood of Issawiya in East Jerusalem became a target for the Israeli army and police. The hope was to break the will of a single man that was incapable of standing on his own feet.

Addameer has enough numbers and figures that would demonstrate without a doubt that Israel has violated every provision of the Third Geneva Convention relative to the Treatment of Prisoners, and every relevant international law. But while there are abundance of numbers, we rarely hear from the Palestinian prisoners themselves.

On the other hand, who doesn't know Gilad Shalit, an Israeli soldier who contributed to the successive raids on besieged and impoverished Gaza. In Western media, Shalit was often portrayed as a victim, a hero, or some other positive or nonthreatening manifestation, but never a killer, or a potential one. Khader, on the other hand was arrested and demonized for "activities that threaten regional security," yet refused a trial, for none was possible with such flimsy pretences.

As for the Palestinian prisoners, who are now 'free', or rather yet to be re-imprisoned, they are the voices of Palestine's finest resisters; they are also the echo of the muted voices of 800,000 Palestinians who had been arrested since 1967, and the millions who are confined behind menacing and expanding walls.

The Prisoners' Diaries are glimpses of the lives behind walls of some of those prisoners, whose existence, pain and heroism cannot be expressed by any statistical evaluation, however thorough, or legal diatribe however indicting. They are loving fathers, like Ibrahim Almasri: "The picture of my two daughters, Omaima and Sojod, gave me the power to bear my life in Nafha Prison and the cruelty of the jailer. It kept my heart beating day by day, despite the daily death the prison imposed upon inmates. It was the hope and solace of my grim life." Or Ahmad Alnajjar: "I always wish to stay in the beautiful world of my dreams, where darkness and chains cannot encircle me. There, I can embrace the innocence of my childhood, with no disturbing voices to steal the pleasure of fatherhood; I can speak and shout freely."

These powerful stories cross the threshold of any casual definition of pain, into a world of hurt unimaginable. Akram Mansor experienced that pain firsthand: "One day, I woke up with a piercing headache. At first I thought it was the result of exhaustion, but the continuous pain did not relent. I tried to avoid it by doing other things, until I could not bear it any longer. Of course, when it came to helping me, the jailers procrastinated and refused to transfer me to the clinic. Finally they allowed me to have a medical examination. The prison doctor hinted that deadly cancer had invaded my head. I did not know what to do. I felt as if someone was trying to suffocate me. I felt the darkness of the prison closing in around me."

But nothing could take away from their humanity; not even many years of separation, and long nights of solitary confinement. "Three decades passed, in which I was burnt by the fire of forcible separation," read the story of Saleem Alkayali. "I missed touching the foot of my mother, who turned 95, and hugging her in my arms. Memories of her still live inside me, and many years of separation have failed to erase them from my mind. My mind was never far from my family, but the many years inside the prison, beginning with my interrogation and extending into the years of my sentence, exhausted my heart and destroyed my youthfulness."

No news reporting, no legal document, no political discourse can articulate the experiences of these prisoners as well as Akram, Ahmad, Ibrahim and Saleem. This book is a noble attempt at bringing to life the true stories of Palestinian prisoners. These stories allow us to live a few of the excruciating moments they have lived, although for them these 'moments' stretched over the course of years and decades. These stories have managed to escape the unforgiving chains of the Israeli jailers. Not only do they represent the experiences of those who are now 'free', but the thousands who remain confined to dark walls, small cells, and the hurt of years to come.

Raed Abu Hammad was found dead on the floor of his cell. But the struggle of his friends and comrades will continue.

- Ramzy Baroud (www.ramzybaroud.net) is an internationally-syndicated columnist and the editor of PalestineChronicle.com. His latest book is My Father Was a Freedom Fighter: Gaza's Untold Story (Pluto Press, London).

Notes:

(1) "Probe death of Palestinian prisoner in Israel jail, PA says." Reuters. April 17, 2010. http://www.haaretz.com/news/probe-death-of-palestinian-prisoner-in-israel-jail-pa-says-1.284441.

(2) "Shalabi's mother: My daughter is dying in prison." Ma'an. March 08, 2012. http://www.maannews.net/eng/ViewDetails.aspx?ID=466199.

(3) Collins, Dylan. "Israel's Farcical 'Compromise' with Hana Shalabi". Palestine Monitor. April 03, 2012. http://www.palestinemonitor.org/?p=4577

(4) Kates, Charlotte. "Israeli Military Courts as Enforcement Mechanism of Occupation." February 23, 2012. Palestine Chronicle. http://palestinechronicle.com/view_article_details.php?id=19122

(5) "See Addameer." http://www.addameer.org/

(6) See page 79

Addameer Prisoner Support & Human Rights Association

Addameer (Arabic for conscience) Prisoner Support & Human Rights Association is a Palestinian non-governmental, civil institution that works to support Palestinian political prisoners held in Israeli and Palestinian prisons.

Established in 1992 by a group of activists dedicated to fighting for human rights, the centre offers free legal aid to political prisoners, advocates their rights at the national and international level, and works to end torture and other violations of prisoners' rights through monitoring, legal procedures and solidarity campaigns.

The centre is based in Ramallah, Palestine.

For more information on Addameer's work visit
www.addameer.org or contact info@addameer.ps

Note

A number of the prisoners' diaries refer to the prisoner exchange that saw the release of Gilad Shalit, the only Israeli soldier held by Palestinians in Gaza, on 18 October 2011, in return for the release of 1,027 Palestinian prisoners.

All the prisoners who dictated these accounts were freed in the prisoner exchange.

Glossary

Abu: father of
Um: mother of
Umi: my mother

A Photograph

Abdulrahman Shihab

I LIVED between strength and weakness, love and hatred, peace and anxiety, the desire to challenge the jailor by showing him how much I loved life and the desire to die – not loving death, but wanting to put an end to the suffering my beloved family had to endure in order to visit me. Conflicting feelings battled in my heart and mind in that damned cell.

I felt intensely sad and happy at the same time. My eyes wanted to close, but my heart opened them again because of thinking too much, which became a source of trouble to me. There was nothing to alleviate my pain but the power of the patience that God granted me as I remembered Him day and night.

On the night before my family visited me, I got ready to meet my father, mother and sister. The next day, all of them came except my mother. We talked briefly but without them telling me why she could not be there. We talked via a telephone cable that barely carried their voices to me. I was standing behind a thick glass barrier which separated my emotions from theirs and prevented me from kissing or hugging my family who I had not hugged or kissed since I was a young man because of the Occupation.

It was a big shock that left me bewildered to hear why

A father on the way to visit a prisoner.

The prisoners are spread over 19 different prisons. All but one are located within Israel, which is not only illegal under international law but also has the practical consequence of making family visits reliant on the issuing of a permit by Israel.

my mother could not come. Missing me so much, she thought of nothing but me. She was hit by a car in front of the prison gate. Her pelvis was broken, and she was hospitalised.

For a month, I got no word of my mother's condition. They were hard times in which I felt no comfort. I wished death could have snatched me before I became a prisoner, exposing those closest to my heart to such dangers and difficulties. I sought death so that they would be released. They would visit my grave once or twice a year. That would be better than being the reason for the suffering they were going through.

I had a visit scheduled two weeks later, but it was put off after I was transferred from Askalan prison to Bir Alsabaa prison. After two weeks, I was moved to the new prison and my father and sister came to visit me. They told me about my mother's health and did their best to convince me that she was okay.

I was looking forward to seeing her as she was being treated in a nearby hospital. I tried many times to visit her, but the prison administration used to put obstacles in my way, repeatedly refusing to allow a visit.

Time passed slowly, 90 days, day after day. My mother appeared one day in a visit that gave me new life, though she was not able to walk well. But her soul was there. Her eyes spoke of her love, making me feel the warmth of motherhood.

My family contributed to the conflicts in my heart. They were my strength, being my only glimpse of hope, making me cling to life harder than ever. They were also my weakness, for I saw the suffering in their eyes every time they visited me.

I always dreamed of hugging my parents. The long years in prison increased my longing to hug them. I was 20 years old when I was arrested and deprived of their wonderful parental love.

In 2004, a concession was made to the prisoners. It allowed prisoners who had parents older than 70 years of age and who were suffering from incurable diseases to take photos with their parents.

I filled in an application to take a photo with my parents that would give solace to my loneliness. The application was refused, for my dad was only 69. I waited one more year. I counted the days and nights. Time passed as slowly as a turtle. It was heavy on me. I submitted my application again. It was accepted and I started waiting for the promised visit.

I was asking myself, what will I do when I meet them?

16 years without touching their hands or smelling their breath. Those days and nights lasted much longer than usual, thinking of the promised day.

My parents came to visit. We talked for 30 minutes then we moved to the next room to meet finally face to face and take a photo. But something weird and horrifying happened!

My father was sweating. He was unable to stand and almost looked like he was fainting. My God, what's happening to my father? What's happening to him, Mum? My mother was talking to me via the telephone cable trying to comfort me. When the 45 minute visit finished the line connecting us was cut automatically, so we tried using sign language.

I started screaming for the jailers and the prison's administrators. I implored them to find a nurse to help my father who looked pale and drained. When the nurse came, he checked my father and summoned a doctor. The doctor came and started checking my dad who became aware of his surroundings, but still could not stand.

When his condition improved a little, we went to the place that had been prepared for taking photos. It was a turning point in my life. I hugged my mother as a young child. Till that moment, I'd thought my mother was taller than I am. I discovered that I was now taller than her. Yes, I had grown up. But, my beloved mother, your position will always be high, as will my father's.

I took a photo, and in the background appeared the clock whose red numerals recorded the time for the end of the visit and the thick glass barrier which had separated us, preventing us from expressing our feelings for many long years. No other prisoner's photo would be like this one.

Today, I am free. I look at the photo without showing it to my parents. I want them to forget the suffering they endured for my sake and to compensate them for the 23 years of deprivation.

Thank God I was freed at last. Praise be to Allah that I live with them today!

Suffocating
The Soul

Ibrahim Almasri

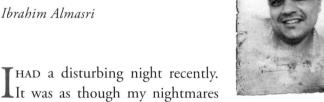

I HAD a disturbing night recently. It was as though my nightmares would hardly allow me to breathe. I awoke sweating and with my heart pounding for no reason. I asked God for forgiveness until I finally fell asleep. But moments later, I woke up again.

On nights like this, I used to seek refuge in a small letter I kept from a visit. I read it until it was in danger of disintegrating, but I didn't care. The picture of my two daughters, Omaima and Sojod, gave me the power to bear my life in Nafha Prison and the cruelty of the jailer. It kept my heart beating day by day, despite the daily death the prison imposed upon inmates. It was the hope and solace of my grim life.

My dears, it's true that I have wasted all the years of your life away from you. I couldn't accept the occupation of my land and home without fighting back. I wouldn't think of sitting lazily and breathing polluted air. Dear Omaima, I can't forget your face as they arrested me 15 years ago when you were two years old; I can't live without your picture. Sojod, forgive me, for I couldn't be with you during the most beautiful years of your life. Now you are older, and I have missed your childhood.

One day I felt my body shaking and my heart racing. I ignored it and kept myself busy, for a prisoner has no other choice.

Something strange was happening in my section of the prison. A group of prisoners was silent, but it was as though words were written on their faces. I thought of urging them to tell me what was going on, but they began speaking in riddles, which they continued for hours. I felt that their speech was directed at me. They talked about life's transience, and about the ultimate reward for patience in our daily lives.

I could not bear this any longer so I asked one of them, "Is there anything wrong that you are trying to hide from me?"

Another prisoner said, "Listen Ibrahim, we know that life inside the prison is different, but it can't be separated from life outside."

"Speak out!" I interrupted him. "What's wrong?"

He mumbled incomprehensible sentences. I couldn't understand any but the last one, when he said, "My deepest condolences, Ibrahim. Your daughter Omaima is in the blessing of Allah."

I felt as if they had stabbed my heart with a dagger. Waves of emotion choked me and scorched my soul again and again, as if they had declared my own death, not my daughter's. How? Why? Where? These questions throbbed inside my head and through my body's fibres.

Oh, Omaima, my first child and light of my eyes, how could you leave without saying goodbye? Now you have become my soul's weariness after you were its life!

Ibrahim with his new born daughter Nour.

I felt dizzy and exhausted. I screamed loudly and hysterically at the people around me. Then memories overwhelmed me. My suffering at the loss of my daughter was greater than my suffering in prison. But the Holy Quran was my solace in my ordeal. I asked God for forgiveness, prayed, and read the Quran. I kept this up for days and months, as if her death was happening daily. I was devastated when I learned from one of my family members during a visit that Omaima had suffered psychologically after the Israeli army broke into our house.

She was shocked by their use of brute force. A month later, she passed away. She had said several times, "Mum, I want to die as a martyr."

I ask God to accept and forgive you.

Hungry For Freedom (Part 1)

Ibrahim Shalash

Six years passed. I counted them day by day and hour by hour. I mentally recalled history books in an attempt to undermine the heaviness of the sentence that would steal 22 years of my life. It is true that I considered these days a sacrifice to God, but freedom is priceless to people like me.

There, in the darkness of Shata jail, we hoped for liberation. We kept alive the thwarted wishes of our youth. We told stories of Hebron's mountains, Ramallah's highlands, Jericho's sea, and Nablus's growing prosperity. Our limitless nostalgia transported us to Acre's walls, Jerusalem's minarets, and Haifa's beaches. In chains, we sought every opportunity for freedom in speech and in writing.

One day I was disturbed by the jailer's shouts. I paced back and forth in the cell, my feet digging into its dirt floor. I gazed into my brothers' faces all around me, then escaped into a world filled with dreams of freedom. I wanted to smash the walls of the prison, bust its heavy iron door, and destroy its floor to escape the jailers' hatred.

Destroy its floor? Yes, I could do it. For freedom is taken, not given. It was worth struggling for, even through layers of earth, dug with my own nails. Such thoughts filled my mind for many hours.

I considered the possibility of escape, drawing close to it boldly then drawing back in fear. Eventually, some brothers and I accepted the idea. We agreed to dig through the floor, looking for freedom.

After long, secret meetings, we decided to dig a tunnel beneath the prison grounds. We knew it would not be easy, and we might pay for it with our lives, but it renewed the commitment for which we had been captured. Its seeds were still in us, and we watered them with our thoughts. We started digging into the floor with our nails and with iron cans. Within a few days, we had succeeded in removing two tiles.

We began the second phase by digging into the concrete without any tools, armed only with an ambition that could breach the walls of any prison. We contrived to keep our work secret. That was very difficult, since our room was next to others. We made noises to deceive the jailer so that he would not realise what was going on. We worked in two teams, one group shouting loudly to cover the sounds of the other group's digging. After long days of painful progress through concrete, we were shocked to find another similar layer of concrete underneath. We agreed not to let this stop us; we would destroy it with our dreams and hopes. We worked with a strange assortment of tools, like the iron blade of a fan, and finally we reached the sand.

Our next challenge was getting rid of the sand! We agreed to throw it down the old toilet next to our room. We planned like engineers. We needed to keep the project secret and finish it as fast as possible.

We finished digging down 2.5 metres then moved away from the tiny window toward the wall. We drew a map to know which direction we should dig. After digging 7 metres toward the street, we built a wooden frame so that the tunnel would not fall on our heads, since trucks crossed the street every day. The lack of air in the tunnel was one of our greatest challenges. We felt exhausted and often came close to collapsing from dizziness. Only our dreams could have sustained this level of courage while we were imprisoned by the Zionists but at the same time seeking our freedom.

Our solution for the darkness was to light three lamps and keep digging and crawling, blessed by God's care. Once, during a routine check, the jailer almost discovered everything we had done, but we deceived him. "His sight was blind, and he returned empty-handed," we said to each other.

You can read the rest of this story in the words of my beloved, freed brother Abbas Shabana in his diary which follows mine.

Hungry For Freedom (Part 2)

Abbas Shabana

THE 'game of courage' we played was a minefield that began with ash and ended with flowers. But nothing we did in prison to relieve our suffering could equal even a moment of freedom. Our dream of freedom was always accompanied by an agony of soul as our imaginations transported us from the darkness of the prison to the light of our stolen homeland.

I'll continue from the point where my brother Ibrahim Shabana stopped while telling the beautiful and terrible story of our prison life. After our efforts to dig the tunnel with primitive tools, we started working our way to the outside wall. I still remember feeling the lack of air while digging, and how it made me so dizzy that I nearly lost my balance. A night later, I laboured from sunset until 2:00a.m, armed with images of freedom and of life outside the prison's living graves.

We succeeded in opening a small gap a few meters from a military watch-tower, and we communicated by certain signs so that we wouldn't alert the watchmen on patrol near the location of our digging. The dream became more real as we got closer to the wall. When the time was right, Ibrahim, another brother and I emerged together from the gap, into the outside air. Walking with quick, light steps, we crossed some metres outside the wall, hoping our dreams were about to come true.

Overjoyed with our liberty, we were surprised by dogs that saw us and started running toward the wall, drawing the soldiers' attention to us. They shone bright lights at us, so we threw ourselves onto the grass, only to discover it was as dry as stones, making a noise that increased the soldiers' suspicions. They surrounded us so quickly we couldn't escape. They encircled us with their guns, and with disbelief, we surrendered. They drew closer to us, already beginning their usual abuse.

We tasted enough torture to send us to martyrs' graves. We hadn't even recovered from the shock of capture when the sticks and rifle butts started hitting us. They left bruises on every part of our bodies, mixed with blood and signed with malice. The painful reminders of that day reached every cell of our bodies. The soldiers took us to their vehicles. We agreed to take responsibility for the operation to avoid implicating our comrades. When they sent us back to the prison, doubled numbers of soldiers awaited us. Each one of us had ten of them waiting to teach him a lesson. They threw us down. Guns again bruised us, and their feet kicked our handcuffed bodies. They attacked us the same way three times, making the already deep wounds on our chests, backs, hands, and legs bleed even more, while denying us any means to defend ourselves.

By then, we could barely maintain our balance. Waves of questions pelted us as they tortured us. But the toughest thing was watching the dream of freedom fade away, remembering that we had been sentenced to life, with little or no hope of freedom.

The measures taken by the investigators were again redoubled after we were sent once again for interrogation, wearing the same muddy clothes for 20 days. They then isolated us in Be'ir Alsab'e, a prison in which sunlight does not shine, for a year. In the end, five months were added to our original long sentences. After that, we were returned to our cells with the description 'dangerous' marked on our cards. But we recognised it as a badge of honour and a story that we will tell our grandchildren, as we remember our eagerness for freedom, not to mention the pain that was born after our hopes were dashed.

By Allah's grace and our fighters' hands, we left the prison with our heads held high and this time not by tunnels. Our bodies embraced freedom with the taste of victory in a way that we will never forget as long as we live.

Abbas Shabana with his first daughter Sidra

Tortured Memories

Sana'a Shihada

I WILL not make any effort to go back to those days, for my mind is full of troubling pictures and painful memories of events that stole years from my life. I was alone and weary, my body was full of pain, and my only strength came from prayer.

On my first day of detention, as is common, I was taken to the Moskobiyyeh Interrogation Centre. It is located in Jerusalem, that is true, but the smell of old streets and dusty stones and the sounds of the call to prayer and the bells of churches failed to reach any of my senses.

Sometimes I would close my eyes and dream of being next to my mother at the al-Aqsa Mosque, where we used to worship. We stood and prayed together in the mosque then lay under the shadow of a tree. The winds lifted the edge of my veil and blew away the last of our exhaustion. The view of the huge stones used to build the house of God inspired me every time I saw them, even though I saw them every day. In the sky, the birds traced random shapes above the domes.

These scenes engaged my imagination, but then I awoke from my daydream and looked around to see darkness and a chair under me, that was used to torture me. There was no window, no air, and no light, except from a tiny bulb strung from the roof of the cell that provided a disturbing yellow glow which brightened and faded from time to time. I longed to see my beautiful room and bed, and I longed to see my Jerusalem and its neighbourhoods full of hope. I uttered words of anger and returned again to the world of memories.

The interrogators didn't differentiate between male and female Palestinian prisoners, as all Palestinians are the same to them. I was tortured the same as the other prisoners. They began by sitting me on a chair, chained for hours, preventing me from sleeping as an army of bugs invaded my narrow room. When it came to interrogations, I was assaulted by a stream of questions and threats, causing headaches that could not be alleviated except by praying and seeking forgiveness from God.

One day, during a round of interrogations, they brought a mobile phone and dialled a number I barely remembered. A woman in her 50s answered. Her voice took me back to childhood when I used to play with my hair. Oh God, did they have enough mercy to let me call my mother? I shouted to her incoherently. She mumbled confusedly, unsure if it was really her daughter or just another trap set by the intelligence service. The investigator silenced me and started threatening her. Then he shook me completely with words I tried not to believe: "We will destroy your house now, so evacuate it immediately."

They sent me back to the cell while I thought of the call and the threats. So this was their plan in calling my mother. I tried to convince myself that it was a crude method by the Occupation intelligence, but my doubts left when they let me listen to another call. The bulldozers had surrounded our house. I could hear my mother's shouting and my father's mumbling in the background as they got ready to destroy it.

How weird is the feeling of confusion when somebody tries to stop my breath and destroy my morale. It is like sculptures being smashed. I wept as I imagined the cruel scene and listened to the voices. My house held memories to me so special that words cannot describe them.

In an instant, hundreds of pictures of the house filled my mind: my room and its beautiful walls, the forecourt shadowed by grapevines, the huge tree with our names carved on its trunk. My father's favourite cane chair, too, and even the old teapot. Every single detail of the house sprang into my mind, bringing nostalgia and sadness together.

My mother's voice asking me not to confess reverberated in my mind when the bulldozers stood in front of our house. She tried to show determination, but her low, thinning voice told another story. I felt guilty and responsible for what was happening, but God inspired me to read verses from the Holy Quran that eased my pain and took away my worry. I stayed like this for days. Only my creator knew about my condition. For days, I fought sleep and drank water to keep myself going. My head felt about to explode from the many questions and thoughts that exhausted my mind.

I learned that my family had succeeded in preventing the demolition order by going to the crooked Zionist courts. At that time, the anger of the interrogators was like snow and peace to me*. I felt the pride of the Palestinians, the glory of Muslims, and the brightness of honesty. I knelt to Allah, thankfully. My tears fell on the floor of the cell, and I am sure they dug a path which those later imprisoned will be able to see.

*An Arabic expression that means "soothing".

The weekly protest at the Red Cross in Gaza every Monday.

Children of Palestinian detainees when they got their school result recently.

Detention Facts and Figures

Since the Israeli occupation of Palestinian territories in 1967, Palestinians have routinely been charged with offenses under Israeli military law and tried in military courts.

Over the last 45 years, more than 800,000 Palestinians have been detained under Israeli military orders in the occupied Palestinian territory (OPT). This equates to around a fifth of the entire Palestinian population in the OPT, and includes much as two fifths of the total male population of Palestine.

While arrests can occur at any time and in any place, Palestinians are most commonly arrested at checkpoints, off the street, at border crossings and from their homes in the middle of the night.

Upon arrest, detainees are usually cuffed with plastic handcuffs and blindfolded. Once bound and blindfolded, detainees may be kept waiting, standing or kneeling, for long periods of time before being thrown on the floor of a military jeep, sometimes face down, for transfer to an interrogation centre.

During the transfer, which can take several hours, Israeli soldiers often abuse detainees. Cases of beatings, kicking, insults, threats and deliberate humiliation are routinely reported.

Palestinian detainees are typically not informed of the reason for their arrest, nor are they told where they will be taken.

Most detained children are subjected to the same treatment.

For more information on Addameer's work visit
www.addameer.org or contact info@addameer.ps

This girl is a daughter of a prisoner, her uncle is a prisoner too and her grandfather was released in the exchange deal of 2011.

Forgive Me, My Daughter!

Ahmad Alnajjar

Our dreams carry us into the mirage of a valley full of expectation. They lead us through the uncertainty of life, increasing our smiles, lessening our pain. I always wish to stay in the beautiful world of my dreams, where darkness and chains cannot encircle me. There, I can embrace the innocence of my childhood, with no disturbing voices to steal the pleasure of fatherhood; I can speak and shout freely.

My story began the night of my arrest, when my mind was on an infant in her mother's womb. She was born without a kiss or even a smile from me to start her life. During her visits, in the presence of the jailers, I was unable to speak, yet it was painful to stay silent.

One day, while I was counting the days of my seven life sentences and crossing them off the accursed calendar, I felt a pain in my throat. It was nothing like the pain that accompanied my tears, or was wrenched from my heart in protest. Even the water I drank and the breezes that blew could not stop it. It increased dramatically until I begged the jailer to take me to the prison clinic, such as it was. I barely got the permit to go. They told me that I was suffering from a malignant disease that had started to spread in my throat. I only said, "Praise and thanks be to Allah!"

Days passed while I thought of my fate, living amongst brutal animals who eagerly wait for the moment when a weakened prisoner falls. I realised that my health would fail in the cells and I asked for Allah's help. I had surgery that removed parts of my throat. I cannot describe the pain I felt. It exhausted my body, and I fought it with prayers, the only recourse I had.

The surgery failed to stop the creeping cancer which had invaded my throat. Screaming in pain, I was threatened by its continued spread.

The easiest thing for the jailer to do was to double my suffering, so he offered me further surgery to silence me. I learned that he wanted to make me dumb. I prayed to Allah. Faith was my food, praise was my shelter, and patience was my weapon. I was like a wounded man telling predators of his pain.

The doctor first told me he would make a small incision, so that I could breathe to stay alive. "Praise be to Allah!" I said. He then came back and told me he would remove my vocal cords. I began crying, because they were my only way to communicate with my family and my beloved ones.

He came back and told me: "We will remove your throat." "Thanks be to Allah!" I said. He came back and said: "We will remove your lymph nodes." "Thanks and praise be to Allah!" I replied. He came back and said: "We will remove your thyroid." "Praise be to Allah!" I said. Then he came and said: "We will move an artery from your chest." "Thanks and praise be to Allah!" I repeated. He came again and said: "We will close the airway between your nose and mouth and open a new one in your lung."

I prayed to my God and said, "There is no God but Allah, and Mohammad is His Prophet." These were my last words.

After I awoke from surgery intended to humiliate me, I imagined my daughter's face. I longed to touch her silky hair, and for her to rest for a moment on my breast. Her next visit was a few days later, when I had no voice. All I had was a gaze filled with tears. I smiled at her, and was inspired by her patience and her innocence. In her eyes, I read words of pent-up anger at the cruelty of the accursed jailer, which embittered her childhood and youth.

I spoke to her using my eyes, and she understood their language. Then tears fell from her eyes and I hugged her. I felt suffocated as the meeting drew to an end. It finished, but my eyes kept sending silent messages of sadness: "Forgive me, my daughter; it's time to leave again."

The Worst Pain Of All

Akram Mansor

T HE night fell heavily on me, filled with pictures and shapes telling a story. My life in prison had been longer than my freedom. It became ever harder, with every single minute full of dark bitterness. In my mind I used to visit Qalqilia's streets and alleys, our calm neighbourhood with the olive tree planted inside it. My thoughts often took me back to the bright smiles of my childhood, away from the jeers of the jailers. I grew sad when I forgot a picture, or when dark images of my imprisonment replaced it in my memory.

I always felt pain when my dreams drifted away from home, the calm sky, the garden walls, and the grass which grew on both sides of the street, only to be replaced by dark walls, the damned metal windows, the canteen, the daily prisoner counts, the "Bursh" (a layer of cotton that we slept on), and the "Bosta" (a van covered on all sides with metal, that transferred prisoners from one prison to another).

One day, I woke up with a piercing headache. At first I thought it was the result of exhaustion, but the continuous pain did not relent. I tried to avoid it by doing other things, until I could not bear it any longer. Of course, when it came to helping me, the jailers procrastinated and refused to transfer me to the clinic. Finally they allowed me to have a medical examination. The prison doctor hinted that deadly cancer had invaded my head. I did not know what to do. I felt as if someone was trying to suffocate me. I felt the darkness of the prison closing in around me.

I suffered in this way for several years, the dizziness and pain in my head increasing. The jailer delayed my examinations to wear me out and kill me slowly. The physical pain in my head grew, along with mental anguish. I didn't want to die between the rusty bars of the prison and to be buried under its solid floor.

My pain led to fainting, vomiting, and seizures, spreading to other parts of my body, its echoes reaching down my neck and beyond. I suffered medical negligence, and I sensed that the jailer wanted to exhaust my soul by delaying the necessary surgery. When he allowed me to have an ear operation, it felt as if he wanted to steal my ability to hear.

The details of those days still fill my memory. The words "blood on your hands" came to my mind when my requests to go to the clinic for immediate treatment were refused. Painkillers were the only remedies I received.

My condition worsened, and fainting set in. A killer does not care about his victim. I felt that I was steps away from death. The jailer used creative methods to torment me -- I felt his hands around my soul, trying to crush it. I decided to go on hunger strike until they offered me proper medical treatment. For four days, illness and exhaustion defined me. I stayed in my bed tasting only bitterness, trying to diffuse the pain throughout my body. At last, the prison staff responded to my demands and transferred me to the clinic, fearing that my voice would be heard in international arenas. I feel proud each time I remember how I forced them to transfer me to the clinic.

There, thanks be to God, I learned that I did not have a malignant disease. The jailer had tried to panic me. It was a wart-like lump on my skin that doubled in size because of medical negligence, causing the fainting and vomiting. I thanked God for His grace and virtue and once again looked forward to life, because I knew I would not be buried in the isolation of the prison's dark walls.

A Stolen Journal

Eyad Obayyat

WHEN a rat* stole my journal from my hands and threw it away, I felt as if someone had stolen my heart. I had kept and protected it like a promise. I loved it as I loved everything attached to my homeland. I used to hold it as tightly as an olive tree guards a memory**. My memories recalled the indescribable; the voices of my brothers whispered to me, "Hold on, Eyad! Don't worry, Abu Mousa." Pictures flashed in my mind. These memories and people lived inside me, and I will never forget them.

On the first page of my journal I recorded my sentence and charge. I did not forget to write my name. I worried that I would mix other inmates' stories with my own. It was three life sentences, and my charge was taking part in killing Zionist soldiers. I used to think that a life sentence equals 25 years, but later I discovered that a life sentence for security prisoners is 99 years. I noted this, put a full-stop, then took a nap while praying to God to decrease my pain and give me patience.

After I had been in prison for two years, my wife came to visit with a painful story to tell. I wrote such stories in the front of my journal. "One day, we were sitting in front of our house as some kids passed with their fathers," Um Mousa said. "Suddenly, Mousa (our six-year-old son) started crying. When I asked him why, he answered, 'Why do they walk with their fathers and I can't?'"

I could not bear to listen to the story; I was dying of pain for this sensitive child.

My children were growing up little by little. After they visited me, I would steal time to quietly write everything new about them in my journal. I used to draw their pictures. I wondered how else time without a father had changed them. How did they look when they came, and when they left? What did we talk about? How many times did they laugh? How many times did they cry? Who occupied my mind most? And who was most affected by my absence?

Grooms asked for my daughters' hands, and they got married. I wrote down the dates and prayed to my God to give them happiness in life. The happiness I felt when I wrote in my journal that I had a grandson, Majd, was indescribable.

Another thought that was always with me in those dark days still resonates in my mind. Amongst us prisoners, the unity of love for our homeland was precious above all other things. It inspired me as nothing else could. I recorded this during the takeover of the Gaza Strip, when the prison authorities separated Hamas prisoners from Fatah prisoners so as to deepen the division between us.

One day, while we were sitting in our section of the prison, we heard chaos outside. It was the sound of Zionists tormenting our brothers in Fatah. So, we started chanting "Allahu Akbar!" in solidarity with our brothers. The rats usually fear our chanting.

Their leader came and exclaimed, "Fatah kills you outside, yet you defend them in here!"

"We are one prisoners' movement," we answered in one voice.

On that day, I wrote a note that I hoped to send to our brothers: "Don't let division distract you from the homeland. The game of division was created by the Zionists."

One day I opened my journal and drew a square around my charge and sentence. I was about to tear the page out, but I didn't. A hidden hand stopped me. Instead I scribbled, "On this day, the judge will bow his head, broken and beaten." This would anger any jailer who read it.

On the same day, I wrote a story about a professional dominoes player in our section, and his nephew in the same section. The professional had finished his sentence and God's relief was about to reach him. His nephew told him, "Come on uncle, the heroes will defeat you today, so that you will never forget them."

Chanting began before we started playing. As we gathered, one of the men said, "Our brothers in Hamas reached a swap deal that will secure the release of 1000 prisoners." The chanting grew louder, and its sound was mixed with tears and congratulations. We smiled, hugged each other, and started to ask who would be included in the deal. We forgot dominoes.

In the last days of my imprisonment, a cowardly soldier said, "Eyad Mousa Salem Obayyat, you will not return to Bethlehem. Rather, you will be punished and sent to the land of death: Gaza."

"To heaven on earth, rat," I replied. "I have family in Gaza. My brother is one of the Church of the Nativity deportees***, and he leads a good life, yet you say 'punished'! God will gather soldiers of truth in Gaza, where you will suffer defeat."

I arrived in Gaza, and my family followed me. They prevented my daughter from coming under the pretext of security. This is the only pain I feel. I miss her, but I am comfortable since she is living with her husband.

Here in Gaza, I am laying the foundations for a new and settled life, amidst Islam and its people, where I feel blessed by God to be alive.

I will buy a new journal to write about life in my beloved Gaza.

---

*   *The prisoners often refer to their tormentors as 'rats'.*

**   *The olive tree is a symbol of history and memory.*

*** *In 2002 Israeli Forces occupied Bethlehem in the West Bank in an attempt to capture Palestinian fighters. Many of the fighters sought refuge in the Church of the Nativity. Eventually, an agreement was reached and they were exiled to the Gaza strip for a year. They are still stuck in Gaza till now.*

A Mother's Anguish

Arina Sarahna

I ENTERED this prison exactly nine years ago on 23 May 2002. I was sentenced to 20 years, although my husband and I had committed no crime. My charge was helping my husband transfer Eisa Bodair to commit a martyrdom operation. Is resisting occupation a crime?

Nine years passed. I counted them day by day, hour by hour, minute by minute. I woke up with the pain of a mother who is far away from her homeland, her family, and her two baby girls. I remembered my two daughters, who were now living in different places. Each of them lived with a different grandmother. Jasmine lived with my mother in Ukraine and Ghazalah lived with her paternal grandmother in Dheisheh Refugee Camp. Drawing pictures of them with my own fingers was my only way to stay in touch with them. They became my companions in the loneliness of the prison, which was filled with the prisoners' longing.

I had not known how much I could stand, or how much pain I could bear in those years – my pain and that of my husband, Ibrahim, who was detained in a cell that was so near and yet so far away, on the other side of a wall that separated us in darkness.

But the ray of light that shone after the Zionist soldier

Gilad Shalit was captured expanded in our hearts and lit the darkness of the cells. It offered us a glimmer of hope that lit my dark life and brought me joy. Ibrahim might be included in the prisoner exchange. We might yet get out to bring to our daughters' cheeks the smiles that had fled years ago.

My name was included. The light I dreamt of every night expanded to open a door to freedom. Then I remembered the people who had sacrificed their lives and won our freedom when they caught Shalit.

I see them running to Heaven. Their brave deeds and pure blood lead them there directly. I smell the perfumed blood of the martyrs. I pray to Allah to open their graves and plant happiness in their mothers' hearts, just as they planted it in my heart.

I remember the day when they offered to send me to Ukraine. To me, that was another sentence. I felt that my rejection of their offer would be a victory, an honour, and a crown to decorate my head. I refused any sentence that would distance me from you, Ibrahim, from my daughters who were impatiently waiting for me, or from the homeland in which I had reached the highest levels of glory. They are my family and my people.

I am a heroine, and the wife of the hero. I chose to stay behind the walls of the cell; I wouldn't go from one humiliation to another. I wouldn't accept a sentence that would have exiled me from my cause. Let me be a witness to the truth, and let me stay here.

But the day of relief was coming. I sat on the bus, a few minutes away from freedom. These minutes felt longer than the ten years I had spent in prison. I stole a look back and saw Ibrahim behind the walls of the prison, as happy as he used to be, sending me his love and some of his pain. I knew that pain as well as I knew him, and it exhausted me as it did him, but by knowing it, I could survive. I could face the Occupation of our homeland that would never grow tired of harassing me. I could bear all sorts of sorrows.

Now I was the one smiling. Soon I would hug my two daughters. For a long time, I had thought that happiness would embrace me one day. My two daughters were older. Would I able to recognise their faces? Would they be able to recognise mine, or had the darkness of the prison changed it?

A smile from their little lips led me, guiding my steps toward them. They wept and cried, yet they looked like two beautiful roses. I hugged their small hands. I kissed them, cried over them, and yelled, looking at the shining light of the sun on the horizon.

Arina Sarahna hugs her two daughters upon her release.

I sent my love to Ibrahim, who knew my pain well. I stood breathing the breeze of freedom. Ibrahim, I send you a promise, covered by my kisses, that I will be waiting for you here. Be patient, Ibrahim; relief will surely come one day.

Detention Facts and Figures

As of 1 January 2013, there were 4,743 Palestinian prisoners in Israeli detention including:

- 178 administrative detainees

- 193 child detainees

- 12 Palestinian Legislative Council members

- 10 women

- 529 Palestinians serving life sentences

- 456 prisoners sentenced to more than 20 years imprisonment

- 111 prisoners arrested before the signing of the Oslo agreements

For more information on Addameer's work visit www.addameer.org or contact info@addameer.ps

'Moskobiyyeh' (Russian Compound), Jerusalem.

Three Decades

Saleem Alkayali

W HEN I arrived in the land of Gaza, pain had spread throughout my body. I felt sad for inmates who were still in the Occupation's prisons. We were released, of course, but we will not forget them, because we know too well the cruelty of the jailer and the prison.

After I was released, I realised that the fence wire was not far from my house in Zeitoun. I wished I could have sent my family a kite bearing my kisses, hoping my kisses would elude the enemies' radar and pass through their barbed wire to reach my loved ones' cheeks.

The toughest time in prison, isolated from the outside world, was when the court of injustice sentenced me to 29 years. On that night, I felt anxious and exhausted. I yawned from lack of sleep. I did my best to sleep to stop the sound of the number 29, which kept reverberating in my mind.

After a while, numbers and words stopped mattering to me. I tried to get used to living this new life. I spent three decades in grave-like prisons, fighting pain, oppression, humiliation, and the misery of missing my family.

Three decades passed, filled with events and memories. They were a sequence of endless pain. I could not see my daughter, who had not been born when they arrested me, because of a jailer had stolen the right to a decent life from me and all the other inmates.

Saleem Alkyali among his family.

Three decades passed, in which I was burnt by the fire of forcible separation. I missed touching the foot of my mother, who turned 95, and hugging her in my arms. Memories of her still live inside me, and many years of separation have failed to erase them from my mind. My mind was never far from my family, but the many years inside the prison, beginning with my interrogation and extending into the years of my sentence, exhausted my heart and destroyed my youthfulness.

I joined the Fatah movement in the 1970s and was arrested in 1976. They sentenced me to three years. I couldn't rest while seeing my beloved Palestine violated.

I went back and formed a military group which killed many Israeli soldiers who had come to Gaza as merchants. They arrested me again and sentenced me and my group's members to life in prison.

We were transferred between prisons often, and I was held in many of them. Their nature didn't change. Sizes might shift, but the jailer is one. What helped me to be patient was the presence of the people of Palestine in this place. We helped each other to be patient, and we eased each other's pain. Our hope was to get out of these small rooms and touch the sand of our homeland.

When the moment arrived, and I heard the news of a deal, I burst into tears. I couldn't control my feelings – it was an unbelievable thing. I lost the ability to express my happiness. I couldn't believe the walls enclosing me had become fragile. Light had entered the dark windows to relieve my heart.

The prison was like a hive that didn't know silence. The prisoners were praying to God to fulfil the deal. I didn't care about the atmosphere surrounding me. Instead I looked at the outside borders of the prison and thought about them. I imagined how my house and my family would be. How would they look after I had been away from them for so long?

I worried about the moment of seeing them. Would I know them? How would they know me? Would I hug them in front of all the crowds waiting in front of our house? Would I feel the old warmth of my family? Many questions filled my mind.

After I arrived home and lived those moments, I remembered the days when I was tortured in prison, in a faraway place whose toughness no one could feel without living inside it. I felt very sad for those who were still inside the prison.

One Night Separates Us

Rawhi Moshtaha

On 13 February 1988, you left your home injured, as you were making a bomb, and you were sent to a cell for 24 years. It wasn't long, Rawhi. It wasn't too much. Do you think that patience shortened the years? If you hadn't had white hair and the ability to count, we would have said they passed quickly, as if they were days. Whether the jailers like it or not, the years passed quickly. I waited for a day that became real at the hands of heroes who fulfilled your trust. People still think of you. Whoever says they forgot our pain is mistaken.

IT is a beautiful deal, as warm to my heart as the patience with which I believed, and with which I climbed high mountains. Nothing could bother me, neither the jailer's punishment nor being isolated in the cells. The Holy Quran was in my hands. I held it tight and smiled. I slept comfortably, and then victory came. It was the victory that lit the darkness of 24 years.

I think of your suffering since our marriage 24 years ago. You were still a bride, and it had been six months since our wedding. You had the same patience I did. I knew then who you were among women, and I am eager to see you now as my freedom draws near.

One night separates me from you. Why won't it end? I ask myself. Is it because it's the last night, Abu Jamal? Or is it simply your eagerness to see a woman who entered your life for only six months, whom you left grasping for patience until she practiced patience beyond what you could imagine? I send you a word, Um Jamal, from my last night in prison: "Allah is great."

How many times did you wake up, Um Jamal, filled with our dreams and memories, wiping tears of loneliness from your cheeks? How many hours did you spend considering the years sacrificed to God? What a great heart you have! What a beautiful belly must have carried you! It's time to meet again, after my hair has turned white and youthfulness has faded away, but my faithfulness, commitment, honesty, manhood, heroism, and sacrifice are still there.

Um Jamal, there is no place in my body that wasn't affected by the blows of the jailer. My eyes still see the darkness of the cells. But your memory never left my body. Your words, the steadfastness in your eyes, and your faithful prayers could heal my wounds. And still I count the days and nights till I see you again. How long can this night last?

I look around as I quit the prison, and I see my fellow prisoners, with whom I have shared one pillow and one dish, remaining behind. We were patient. My heart is full of pain, yet I look forward to the one I love. So I smile despite the sadness nesting at the bottom of my shattered heart.

As I am moved from one section of the prison to

another, I seek more patience. Among all the thoughts of my heart, resistance, freedom and victory are still the greatest. I will carry them on my shoulders for the rest of my life, until they are achieved.

Do you still remember, Um Jamal, when I told you to end your marriage with me and start your own life again? Do you remember what you said? "I will wait for you until the last day of my life." My mounting admiration for you spurs me to imitate your patience and power, so that my strength comes to equal your own.

Now I am getting down from the prisoners' bus at the Rafah Crossing. My hands shake as my feet take their first steps in the land of freedom. I look for your face among the crowds. I smile as you stand before me, strong and patient.

You give me a military salute, then fall into my arms, casting aside the pain of 24 years, strong, patient, and awaiting God's reward.

I know that you are the finest woman in the world.

Rawhi Mushtaha with his brother after 32 years.

What A Place To Be Sick!

Ibrahim Joundia

WE lead a difficult life inside these prisons. Outside, when a person suffers from illness, you can see it on his face, and when he asks others to help him get medication, they do. But in prison, it's completely different. I suffered very much there. When a prisoner feels ill, he must be strong, even if it results in his death, rather than giving the jailers any opportunity to humiliate him or to gloat.

The times that I spent in interrogation rooms were very hard, but I did not expect what came next to be still worse.

Soon after I left the interrogation rooms to begin serving my prison term, I started to feel pain in my feet. It was hard at first. I tried to be silent and relax, but I couldn't bear it.

I was in prison, and the prison clinic is not there to decrease pain, but rather to increase it. This, in addition to the bad treatment imposed on us, worsened the suffering of any prisoner who sought medical care.

A drowning man will clutch a straw. My pain kept getting worse, and I could not remain patient anymore, so the prison clinic was my last glimmer of hope.

I went to the clinic and met the physician. He said apathetically, "You haven't got any pain." He meant that I was okay, and was lying to him. He refused to diagnose me or to transfer me to a hospital or clinic to learn what was causing my pain.

Eventually, I lost the ability to walk and needed help to move around the prison. I could not get water when I felt thirsty. I was unable to stand up to pray like other inmates, to go out when we were allowed recreation, or to walk so as to boost my circulation. I could not even go to the toilet.

These were hard times. My brothers moved and ran, although they were imprisoned, but I could not. I was a prisoner of both my cell and my inability to walk. The prison physician eventually gave me some drugs, but only to alleviate my pain.

My condition became worse. Under increasing pressure from other inmates to give me medication, the prison service finally transferred me to Al-Ramla Hospital. I will not narrate the details of my journey now, but it was full of pain and humiliation beyond description. The physician who examined me was very surprised at how drastically my condition had deteriorated due to negligence over the last three years.

I started to tell the doctor about my condition. He interrupted, telling me that he couldn't deal with my type of case. I stayed in Al-Ramla Hospital for two months. During this time, other doctors cured me, and I regained my ability to walk.

After that, I went back to my prison, glad to see my brothers and to walk again.

I was once more doing everything for myself without any help, but the Occupation continued to humiliate prisoners and kill their happiness.

A year later, the same problem recurred, and I went again to the hospital. After that, the prison staff stopped my treatment.

I realised then that they wanted to humiliate me, not cure me, so I decided to help myself without relying on them. On my brothers' advice, I started to exercise and lose weight.

I succeeded and regained the ability to walk normally with less pain. And in this way I became an example of steadfastness and defiance in the face of the jailers' arrogance and the oppression of the prison service.

A New Grave

Obada Belal

MANY days and hours filled my memory and refused to fade away. The years of longing for my homeland and everything about it fed my silent pain. My years in prison brought nothing but sorrow and shattered smiles.

Among the millions of minutes that make up my life I can now recall only those spent in Asqalan prison, where I came to know the literal meaning of the words "earthly grave", and where the pain of aggression is made worse by the hatred of the jailer.

There, one tale contains all the others: death, and nothing else. There I learned how misery crushes any attempt to smile.

I was in Eashel prison's isolation when they decided to transfer my brother Ahmad Almoghrabi and me to Asqalan's isolation*. To me, it still meant isolation. They chained all the parts of our bodies, including our fingers. They checked us more times than I could count. I felt the impure hands of the soldier checking every part of my body. His breathing penetrated my ears. I tried to stay away from him because of my anger and terror. Although my blind eyes couldn't see him, I drew a mental picture from his noisy voice and movements. He is only a soldier brought from South Africa's forests, Europe's beaches, or

Russia's frost, I thought.

I didn't care about him, but I cared about what he might be doing as I felt him moving around me. We had travelled to Asqalan prison sitting on the Bosta's cold, hard chairs. The van's motion made me feel like vomiting, but I tried to keep from doing so by praying. Finally, we arrived at our new isolation cell. After tedious procedures that lasted for hours, we entered our cells hoping for some relaxation after our painful trip. But Ahmad's voice started to change as we got into the room. I didn't know why. Sometimes, being blind can be a blessing. Ahmad didn't want to worry me, and he started checking the so-called room.

I walked forward and collided with a wall. Then I walked a few steps to the left and collided with another. Finally, I walked to the right and collided with Ahmad. I asked him with surprise, "Where are we?"

"In a new grave," he answered ironically.

It took us only moments to check the room. We were to live in a cement box with a small metal door, in which human beings called 'prisoners' are kept. My blindness added to my pain. Every time I moved, I was in danger of bumping into the things in the cell. During the twenty days that I spent with Ahmad in Asqalan, I felt time moving ever slower, while the senses of weariness and isolation grew stronger. I spent most of my time reading the Holy Quran, praying, and asking for forgiveness and blessing. I would leave my lethal chains by thinking of my four brothers, scattered in four other prisons.

Sometimes I allowed myself to remember Nablus, its neighbourhoods and narrow streets and the yard of our huge house. In the shrinking grave of my cell, I clung to memories of its size. I inwardly cursed the prison while also thanking God for testing me.

I tried to endure the sufferings caused by the jailer so that they would be counted as good deeds on the Day of Judgment. The guards cursed Allah in front of us many times, and forced us to listen to their cursing. We felt as if our souls were leaving our bodies, and guilty at having to listen to blasphemy. I felt only sadness as I sat on what might be called a bed, repeating, "God, forgive me, I have nothing but tears."

Those days were really hard and painful, of course, but Ahmad changed them to a heaven in which the spirit of brotherhood rose above more trivial things. He was like a passionate mother, always worrying for me. He would nudge me when I was about to hit something, and he helped me eat my food.

He would break our isolation with his beautiful words. He took me to another world that the jailers could never understand. We travelled together to a world of honesty, where the theories we had learned about brotherhood or friendship were proven true. We strengthened ourselves to do good deeds. We waited for the creator's reward for our suffering. This lasted until a new isolation distanced us and tried to crush the life from us**. We could only face it by kneeling and praying with patience and thanks.

---

*   *The two men were incarcerated together, probably because one of them is blind.*

**   *They were later separated.*

The Light Of Freedom

Alaa' Albazyan

I ARRANGE my things. I touch my clothes and case, and I collect my remaining memories, which have become part of me and refuse to leave. Despite the breezes of freedom, I touch my face and count the wrinkles that increased every year in prison. Then I forget to count them. I no longer care about numbers. All of them mix together in my heart, which was inflamed with defiance and resistance in the spring of my long years. The sun shines, then it disappears. It is the sunlight that shone upon and released the birds of freedom. They now fly above my heart full of pain and memories of waiting. They scatter in the sky, to be replaced by tears of happiness. It is relief – believe it, Alaa'!

From here, from that brutal window, I saw my mother's funeral passing. One year ago, my mother was covered with sand. I hug her as in an old dream. Then my father's funeral passed the same way. Only a few months separated their burials, and they are together in a peaceful spot, their longings buried with them in the ground of old Jerusalem. I imagine them, my mind filled with longing, without seeing them, without any words of farewell. Two tears fall from my eyes, and my grieving heart heaves again. But still there is hope.

I turn back to my case and recall the past, 25 years ago. A bomb occupies my memories and a cell reinforces my steadfastness and pride. I remember lying on a bed at Hadasa

Alaa' Albazyan at his wedding party.

Hospital, where I lay covered in blood after the bomb I was carrying exploded, and I lost my sight. My body was laid on the floor of the hospital. They moved me mercilessly, wounded and blind, chained by iron, to be tortured in a prison where wounds meant nothing.

They are 25 years out of my life. Today I leave my grave and return to life. Prison was as bad as death. Memories reopened old wounds, hurting me, and adding insult to my injuries. The jailers' cold water was poured on my naked body, making it shake and shudder, but then grow stronger.

It is not merely a dream that I am collecting my things now. Relief is finally in sight, Alaa'. Tomorrow, I will sit beside my parents' graves, complain of my pain, and share the happiness of freedom and victory. Tomorrow, I will acquire power from them to return again to life. Alaa', life is freedom. I am not used to tasting freedom. Now I see it too late. Nothing is left from the memory of prison except a sick body, blind eyes, and black memories.

But there is also a glimpse of hope, from which I will start.

Family visit

Detention Facts and Figures

All but one of the prisons where Israel detains Palestinian
prisoners are located inside Israel, in direct contravention
of Article 76 of the Fourth Geneva Convention, which
states that an Occupying Power must detain residents of
occupied territory in prisons inside the occupied territory.

In addition to illegality under international law,
the practical consequence of this system is that many
prisoners have difficulty meeting with Palestinian defence
counsel, and do not receive family visits as their attorneys
and relatives are denied permits to enter Israel on
"security grounds".

*For more information on Addameer's work visit
www.addameer.org or contact info@addameer.ps*

Damon prison, northern Israel

Ofer Prison & Military Court, West Bank.

Prison Isn't Built On The Shoulders Of Men

Ali Alamuodi

I HUNG in the air by my feet as blood dripped from my body. My jacket was covered with blood. My whole body was exhausted and weak. I felt numb as shrapnel penetrated my body. A few hours before, I had been in a military clash in Abu Dees, near Jerusalem, which continued for seven hours. My beloved brother, Abed Alrahman Hamdan, was martyred. An old man sat near me in the prison. I was less than 24 years old.

He looked at me and asked, "Who are you?"

"There is no change nor strength except through Allah, to Allah we belong, and to Him we will return." I replied using these words each time he asked a question, for I was very afraid to speak to him, fearing he could be an infiltrator. I knew this man later. He was a great one.

One month later, the Occupation court sentenced me to three lifetimes in prison. I had taken part in killing Noaim Kohain, the Shabak commander in Gaza and the West Bank, in an operation that shook the foundation of the Israeli enemy's intelligence. This could not have happened without God's grace. I spent 18 years in prison. I was released under 'The Promise of the Free' agreement.

In court, the judge rapped the table as he declared my sentence. He didn't shake a single hair on my body. The homeland is bigger than I am. Challenging my enemy, I smiled and crossed the gate back to prison. At the gate of the court, one of the officers saw me and told me in Hebrew, "Prison isn't built on the shoulders of men."* I understood what he said. Hours, days and years passed. Today we will leave after 18 years. The chains were broken, and we survived. Prison isn't built on the shoulders of men!

As soon as I heard about the deal, I started collecting my things. I raced against time as I had none to lose. My eyes saw nothing except freedom and freedom alone. I spent 18 years in the cells and blocks of the prisons. I couldn't see my parents and family for eight of those years. Today, it's time to meet them.

My brother called me via a mobile phone smuggled into the prison. He asked about the projects I have in mind after my release. "I don't want anything," I said. "I don't look for anything but freedom. Don't talk to me about getting married or getting a job or completing my studies. Just talk about freedom, only freedom," I said.

When I left prison and hugged my family, my entire life changed. How beautiful! Who is this, and whose son is that? And whose daughter is that? Children whom I don't know, kids who were young when I left are now parents. They introduced their kids to me. This is Maisa, this is Ghaida, and that is Ali. These are Ibrahim, Ahmad, and Salim.

A few days after my release, my father brought fish for lunch. It was very expensive. In our house in Khan Younis, there were tens of cats. I put a fish in front of a cat. It ate the fish and nudged my hand with its head.

I laughed. My father looked at me and said: "You feed the cat this expensive fish!"

"Yes, nobody knows the meaning of freedom except those who have lost it," I said.

The days of prison were very hard. I hope they don't return.

---

* *This means they will not stay in prison forever.*

Out Of The Depths

Forsan Khalifa

In the darkness of the Occupation prisons, men and women were full of youth. We were all forced to live there, in a world where we could see nothing but darkness. Its sky was dark with no stars or moon. Its day was dark as its night. Its land was narrow. Its air smelled foul. In brief, it was a world that stole the spring of our youthfulness.

Let me tell you about my experience in the cemeteries of the living. I am Forsan Khalifa from Aien Shams Camp. I was arrested on 17 April 2003 for my involvement in the Al-Qassam Brigades – the military wing of the Hamas movement – and for helping two young men reach their destination to blow themselves up deep within the lands that the Zionists have occupied since 1948. I was sentenced to 20 years.

During my incarceration, I was moved to various prisons, where the jailers meted out only humiliation and degradation. I had brothers in other sections of the prison, like my brother, an Islamic Jihad member in Section 7, and my other brother, a Fatah member in Section 2. I was in Section 5 of Ramon prison. We never met. We are brothers, but the prison separated us, as if each of us came from another planet. The prison service was run by the occupying force, men with no senses or emotions.

The walls of the prison did not set any value on the human soul. They contained only pain and groaning. Behind the bars, we felt the pangs of disease in our chests, which tightened in dark rooms under brutal jailers. Our secret tears strengthened our souls when we needed support that we could not find outside ourselves.

But this ordeal proved to be a gift. The prison turned into a land of limitless joy as we stormed its walls and passed its military fence. There was great news: the Palestinian resistance had succeeded in completing an honourable swap deal and making our jailers bow to its terms. One Zionist soldier was exchanged for hundreds of Palestinians serving tough sentences in those abhorred prisons.

Since 2006, our hopes had ebbed and flowed as we heard news of a potential deal. The Occupation often broke or blocked its agreements. They wanted to crush our morale. We no longer trusted any news about a deal until we found ourselves finally leaving the prison walls.

While waiting and hoping, we were sure that a deal would be reached, especially after the last Zionist war on the Gaza Strip in 2008-2009 and the Occupation's failure to retrieve its soldier. Hamas performed an amazing feat in keeping Schalit and not giving up.

On the eve of fulfilling the deal, we watched the news on a TV channel we didn't trust at all. The breaking news was too familiar to us – we were used to hearing false news on that satellite channel. It had broken the hearts of prisoners many times before by broadcasting false reports. We changed the channel and saw the same news on a different station, but still we felt doubtful. We were allowed to watch only five TV channels, including two news channels and three music stations which we never watched at all. What finally made us sure was seeing the head of the political bureau of Hamas, Khalid Masha'al, announcing the success of the deal. At that moment, we knew that freedom was very near.

A moment of absolute silence fell over us. Then we burst into chanting: "Allah is great!" "Praise be to Allah!" We knelt to Allah, hot tears falling from our eyes heavily and unconsciously. Doubt turned into hope as Masha'al spoke. Soon, we didn't have a shadow of doubt that the breaking news was true and that the moment of our freedom was close.

Then the entire planet was not enough to contain our happiness. We felt that we had defeated the jailer, who had always given us water from the cup of humiliation and bitterness. We felt a desire to break the chains and the iron doors. The tears we shed as we hugged and left our beloved brothers in prison were truly the toughest ever. We were like one family with different mothers.

Before we got out, we wrote tearful letters to those we left behind. We distributed clothes and belongings and stayed awake praising and thanking God. Our souls were reborn in our bodies. Our senses were confused. We waited a long time for truth, but when it came, it felt like everything we had imagined.

Before departure, they took us to the security administration department to make sure of our names and to sign for our belongings and medical files. They checked our DNA, and confirmed our information by having seven officers from behind seven separate tables repeat the same questions.

They brought us a paper to sign that said: "We agree to reject violence against the Occupation." The most dangerous item stated that the courts had a right to add our old sentence to a new one if we were sentenced again. That clause was dropped after the prisoners tore it apart. We signed another paper stating that we accepted the prisoner exchange agreement.

We reached the last stage: meeting the intelligence commander, who put the final touches on our files. When I arrived to meet him, he informed me that I had a mistake in my name. Instead of writing "Forsan", they had written "Farhan"! This was certainly wrong. I answered that fool of an officer, saying, "You Zionists always make mistakes." We started a long and hot debate.

"We arrested your brother immediately after his wedding party. He has been in prison for 20 days," the officer said, trying to provoke me.

"I don't care, it's a normal thing," I replied. I was worried and distracted, so I refused to argue with him, even though I felt that dignity and honour demanded it.

"In Judaism, we say you are bastards," the officer said. Provoked, I answered him angrily: "The bastards are those who stole my land."

"What do you mean?" he demanded. I replied, "Anyone who stole my land, whether a Jew or a Palestinian."

That drove him mad. He told me, "You're rude."

"I'm polite, but your questions aren't," I retorted.

"It seems you didn't learn your lesson in the prison," he said.

"No, I did," I replied. "Now I will go back to Gaza."

"How many years did you spend in prison?"

"Nine years," I said.

"Next time, your sentence will be longer."

I replied, "If there is a next time."

"If you do anything wrong in Gaza, we will fire a missile at you.

"It's a martyrdom we all long for," I answered.

"We don't wish you martyrdom," he said. "We hope your hands and legs get blown off and you stay alive."

At the end, I wanted to conclude by provoking him. "I want to tell you something. Jaser Albarghothi is standing behind me. If you remember, he killed 17 soldiers. You swore that he would never again see the light of day, and that he would return to his family in a black bag. Now what is he doing? He's standing behind me, for you to sign his release! You don't keep your promises. You talk too much."

Then he shut up, not uttering another word. There was nothing he could do but to sign all the papers of the released prisoners.

The Day My Children Were Scattered

Kahera Als'adi

Y days passed like dreams. My soul and my breathing were weak as I remembered the stolen past and imagined a beautiful future yet to come. I stayed in Moskobiyyeh prison. My frail body withstood an army of interrogators. If I described them as stones, I would be unjust, for even stones sometimes soften.

A small chair and filthy walls were all I had in a cell barely larger than I am. The dyspnea that choked me wasn't a sickness or a pain as much as a longing for the landscape of life outside this living grave. I defied them many times and forced myself to conceal my tears. I thought only of my four children whom I had left behind and who were snatched away from me.

When my mind succeeded in leaving that dark room, it would fly to Sandy innocent's face, Mohammad's childhood, Ra'fat's features, and Donia's hair. They, their names and images never left my heart. I never forgot my four children who eased my body's pain even as torture covered me in bruises.

Their pictures in my mind's eye gave me the patience to endure the bitterness of my interrogation, which lasted three months. When my chained feet lost their feeling, I imagined I was cooking their food in our warm house. As jailers prevented me from sleeping for hours, I remembered the moments of their lives, and how they enriched my own. Even when my interrogators threw me to the floor, trampled me underfoot, and covered my body with the signs of torture and racism, I left them behind by praying and shouting to be where I wanted to be: among my four children.

A year passed, and I saw no trace of them. My many questions drove me to madness. Where were they? With whom were they staying? I worried especially because my husband, his brothers and I had all been arrested on the same day, without any of us being able to make sure that the kids were okay. I was another person, not Kahera. Although my name means 'vanquisher', I felt defeated, miserable and wounded, and I was desperate to see my children, even from far away.

A year later, I was told that two of my children were going to visit me. This news made my spirit fly into the sky, casting aside everything that constrained it. Something inside me, though, grabbed my heart. I felt it was the longing to see them, but as the visit came, I knew what it was. I looked at my two innocent children, full of questions, behind a dirty iron-barred window. I wiped the glass with my clothes, thinking I hadn't recognised them yet. My mouth fell open with surprise. When I saw their faces, I remembered our beautiful past.

They were my children Mohammad and Ra'fat. They were older, and so sad they were crying. I asked them to be calm, and not to make my tears fall. "Don't worry, I'm here, I'm okay." My words increased their river of their tears and cries. Oh my God, what had happened to them? And why did they look like this, as if they didn't have a house to live in?

During the short moments of their visit, I learned from them that they

Kahera Als'adi with her two sons

had lived in an orphanage since my arrest. They didn't know where their two sisters, Sandy and Donia, were, since they had been taken to another orphanage. This drove me mad. During my detention, I had imagined my four children living in the house of one of our relatives. I couldn't keep myself from bursting into tears. Was my loving family scattered like this? Was fate against us because of our love for our homeland?

When I realised that the visit would end soon, I shed more tears, wiping my eyes on a sheet. I mumbled sentences to make my children feel easier and more comfortable, assuring them that the coming days would bring better fortune. I said things to raise their spirits and make them feel better about my condition, however bitter it was. They smiled at me, kindling new life in my heart.

We awoke from these beautiful moments when the voice of the officer announced the end of the visit. I saw them off as if I were losing a part of my body. I waved my hands, my eyes gazing into theirs, trying to follow them as far as possible.

After the visit, I felt like a slaughtered sheep. They sent me back to the prison, a body without a soul. I entered my room, my condition worse than it was before the visit. I tried to sleep on my bed, but the inmates started asking me dozens of questions about my children. I looked at them and fell down on the ground, dizzy to the point of unconsciousness, remembering the voices of Mohammad and Ra'fat crying. I kept repeating their names as moans of pain left my breast, complaining to Allah about the injustice of the oppressors.

A Brother's Love

Mazin Foqha'a

I REMEMBER the day when I stopped breathing. I hastily began praying to God to make that day a good one. A few moments later, I heard news so bad it made me collapse despite my continuous steadfastness for the six years I had been living between prison walls – walls that were breached only by my patience and hope for freedom.

How difficult it was when I received the news that my brother Ahmad had been taken to hospital! Someone from outside the prison told me, "Pray for Ahmad. He could pass away within hours. He is between death and life."

These words, Ahmad, made me think thousands of times about the thalassaemia you suffered from.

I resisted Satan when he told me: "You had better insist that your father not allow Ahmad to go to Saudi Arabia to perform Umrah." I felt powerless and wanted to melt the iron of the prison and walk to where you were, in a hospital in Saudi Arabia, to touch and kiss your face for the last time.*

That night filled me with fear. I couldn't sleep. I resisted it so that news of your death wouldn't fill my rest with nightmares. I promised you I wouldn't cry in prison, but news of your sickness suffocated, weakened, and pained me despite my brothers' soothing words about their prayers for you.

You know, Ahmad, when I used to hear my mobile, which was hidden from the eyes of the prison department, ringing, my heart would stop, as I readied myself for news of your death. My feelings were confused.

I lived on a memory that provided me with hope. When you were a kid, aged six, I carried you to the hospital for a blood transfusion. You entered a coma in my arms. Then you came back to life. On that day, my hope for your speedy recovery was restored.

In prison, I used the time after other inmates went to bed to remember my beautiful days with you, when I used to take you to the countryside to ride your bicycle. And I remembered the pain of our mother, who lived in Tubas and worried about you when we stayed away from home.

I lamented the days that hurt me. My painful doubts and dreams haunted me, especially when I remembered my brother Moa'th, who was years younger than me and who had died of the same disease.

At the time, I blamed myself for refusing to fix his bike the day before his death because I was busy at the university. I began to fear, Ahmad, that I would not carry out my promise to buy you a car when I got out of prison.

I asked for forgiveness and prayed to God to heal you. A few days later, I heard the news of your recovery. I felt so happy because hope had returned to me.

Finally, when you have healed and grown older, I will

breathe freedom with you. I will compensate you for all the days when you missed me. I will tell you the stories I lived in prison and you will be my close friend, my dear brother.

Mazin Fogha'a giving a talk about prisoners.

---

* *Mazin Foqha'a's brother had gone to Saudi Arabia for Umrah (a pilgrimage to Mecca that can be undertaken at any time of the year) despite their father's objection. The brother fell sick with thalassaemia while performing Umrah and had to be hospitalised.*

Detention Facts and Figures

- 800,000 Palestinians arrested since 1967

- 75,000 arrested since the beginning of the Al-Aqsa Intifada

- 2,000 cases of torture in 2008 alone

- 645 complaints of torture and ill-treatment submitted against ISA interrogators between 2001 and late 2010

- Not one criminal investigation initiated

- Between March 2002 and October 2002, 15,000 Palestinians arrested in mass arrest campaigns

For more information on Addameer's work visit www.addameer.org or contact info@addameer.ps

A model of the Dome of the Rock made from toothpaste tubes by a Palestinian political prisoner whilst being held in prison by Israel. Gaza, Palestine.

Search And Suppression

Mohammad Alderawi

THE cell turned into a beehive whenever something happened. Two or three human beings are confined in each cell, in a space utterly unlike the outside world we have lost. The size of the cell is less than four square meters, including the toilet and the water tap. It is used to live, sleep, and do some exercise. The foul smell rising from its filth would keep you from coming too close. What about a man who has lived here and nowhere else for days and months?

The bugs that came out of the toilet were the only proof that there was life beyond these walls. The jailers who wore the clothes of the living were dead. Their sour faces no longer held any life.

The time got closer to the call for the Alfajr (dawn) prayer. As always, everybody was preparing himself to perform this prayer. It gave us tremendous energy, helping us to penetrate cell walls to reach a wide world full of Allah's love. We sought His forgiveness, and that brought relief, easing years of pain at the hands of the Zionists.

Silence filled the room, except for whispered requests for forgiveness, recitation of the Holy Quran, and the footsteps of soldiers who stayed awake and moved from one place to another. Suddenly, I heard loud voices that I didn't recognise because, at that time, I was a new prisoner in the Occupation jails. My companions told me it was the voices of soldiers who carried out search and suppression operations against the prisoners.

I don't deny that I was waiting to see what would happen, for I had no experience of such a thing. What would they do? What do they suppress? And why at this very early hour? Many questions arose in my mind, and my heart started racing. I had no preparation except for the description of those who had experienced this before. Now I was destined to live through it myself. Voices drew closer, and the sound of many footsteps revealed that dozens of soldiers were walking down the passages between the cells.

They started opening the cell doors and shouting. Violent clashes began between the weakened prisoners – exhausted from lack of sleep, the narrowness of the cells, the coldness of the walls and the filth of the floors – and the soldiers, who were armed to the teeth.

More than five soldiers entered my room. They opened the metal door that always stood between us and the beauty of life. One of them shouted at us, ordering us out of the room which they turned upside down, as if they were looking for a needle in a haystack.

They asked us if we had concealed mobile phones inside the cell. We denied having any, so they became very angry and ordered us all out into the extremely cold weather, where they strip-searched us.

Some of you may think that being strip-searched is a trivial matter. It is not. It is a humiliating experience, full of suffering and degradation. I felt so humiliated and degraded that I shouted at the officers, threatening to stab one of them in retaliation.

They sent us back to the cells and closed the metal doors again before sunrise. They left frustrated – although they had terrorised us, they had failed to find mobiles in any of the cells.

Mohammad Alderawi with his five-day old boy Emaad Al-Deen.

My Son, My Son

The mother of freed prisoner
Marwan Alzard

THE wrinkles on a face record life's painful histories like cracks in a great building. The wounds open from time to time, bleeding with longing, breathing the pain of separation, and lamenting the tragedy of grieving motherhood and of thwarted hopes.

I look at my face in the mirror to see Marwan standing behind me, suddenly hugging me tightly and patting my shoulders. He pulls me to himself lovingly and carries me to a great castle of happiness. "On this blessed night, our dear Marwan is visiting us, being wedded to freedom in a glittering ceremony at the beach of glory and joy," is written on the castle gates.

I can't believe what I see, nor can I stop myself from shedding a tear, as I have often nearly done before. I touch the shoulders of the man who is standing next to me, then his chest and his face. I touch his hands to make sure that he is Marwan. I read in his eyes the twenty years that have passed without him. But I only cried a single tear.

It is no surprise to see him in my dream, for the time is drawing closer. It is the day in which my dream will come true, to see my son free at last, as a lofty lion. It is the day towards which my heart has flown, and I cannot help but rejoice. I am the freed groom's mother.

Oh brave lion, I would sacrifice my heart to save you. I would give my soul and every valuable thing to free you. My imagination could not offer me a picture of my beloved patiently enduring behind the walls of humiliation. But my imagination was weaker than God's will, which always allowed me to see him in my dreams as if I was with him the whole night.

I recalled my precious son growing day by day. When Marwan (or Ibrahim, as everyone calls him) turned 17, I was happy for his early manhood – his confident, trusting breath; his way of talking and dealing with others; even his loves and hates.

When I saw him carrying his gun, I remembered his childhood and teenage years. I imagined him as a great and glorious man.

Poverty and oppression invaded my house. Grandsons of monkeys got into my house and stole my beloved, the soul of my heart, leaving me burning with the pain of separation. They would not give me permission to go and see him, nor would they heal my soul from its deadly longing.

When a Mujahid (fighter) is captured at a young age, the heart of his mother burns for him, because he still needs her and his family more than an older man would, but Marwan soothed me. He knew that I needed him as much as he needed me.

Every night, he visited me in my dreams. I would tell him, "You are part of my heart. Are you ok?"

"Please Mum, be fine, so that I can be ok," he replied. "Give me a blessing that will warm my cold nights. You have the purest heart on earth. Your words calm me. Do you miss me that much, Mum?"

"More than much, my heart," I said.

"I pray to Allah to save and take care of you," he concluded. "Peace be upon you, my patient mother!"

Marwan was still very young when the Zionists arrested him. I worried that they would hurt him. I knew that my son was a lion wearing the clothes of a kid. But I wasn't frightened, despite the possibility of them harming him, for Allah is the best guardian.

I wished to see my son growing up before my eyes, to see his features and feel his bones growing, for his muscles to tell me that he was becoming a man. To see his shoulders getting broader. To watch his legs, his hands, and even his easy smile, his beard and moustache growing on his bright face. To see his neck swelling with anger but never bowed under the weight of its chains. But, adding insult to injury, the Zionists never allowed me to see him after his capture.

I started praying to Allah more and more not to deprive me of the sight of my son. I started seeing him in my dreams. Until each morning, I would see his familiar features while he visited me each night. He was the same son I knew.

When Jewish Rabbis issued an edict that allowed burning Israel's prisons with their Palestinian prisoners inside them, a young journalist visited me and asked if I really thought that they would carry out this threat. I answered confidently, though my heart was burning, "No, my friend, Allah will keep them safe."

I imagined the day when Marwan would come back

to me. My heart wouldn't be able to bear the joy of his return, and would start burning again. Allah soothed my heart, even when my son became stubborn and didn't want me to go and meet him in Al Kateeba Square, but I too became stubborn and went there to receive him.

I touched his whole heart and soul when I hugged him on the day of his honourable release. I memorised even the number of his breaths and heartbeats. Oh Allah, You were good to me!

Now, many people whom I have never met or known are coming to congratulate me. And though I feel the ravages of disease invade my body, I don't care. My heart lives its best days near my beloved. My soul is being washed by the rivers of his joyful and gentle kisses. I look into people's eyes and pray that Allah will warm the hearts of all families still waiting for their prisoners to get out, still living under the aggression of the Occupation.

A Martyr

Wafa Albis

IT was the worst moment of my life. I felt distress and despair like never before. One of my cherished dreams ended today in the twinkling of an eye.

Instead of going to paradise, God willing, I went to a Zionist cage. A female soldier came to me and said angrily: "You came here to kill innocents and children in Israel, terrorist?"

"I am a martyr no matter what you do," I answered immediately. In front of me, they detonated the explosive belt I had been wearing under my dress and veil.*

On that day, the Hebrew media, including satellite channels and radio stations, invaded to take photos of me. I felt as if I were an expensive trophy, and so I was to them. The soldier who captured me was rewarded, although he was more lucky than smart.

They interrogated me. Three female jailers struck me on the injured parts of my body with their iron sticks. This lasted for almost 15 minutes and caused unbearable bleeding and pain.

I was tied Guantanamo-style. They asked me about the faction that sent me, but I didn't confess, for confession was treason to me. They sarcastically asked if I felt regret, but I answered, no. Every time I denied feeling regret, they hit me more, until I lost consciousness, finally waking in a cell unfit for human life.

They gave me some medical aid to stop the bleeding and heal my broken fingers. That was in Ramallah's isolation, the most horrible one. A week later, the martyr Hassan El-Madhoun, a Fatah military leader, acclaimed my action on television.

While I was interrogated for three months, I saw nobody but the criminal jailers who threatened to rape me. That was my worst nightmare.

After that, the physical torture ended. They removed me to the next stage: psychological and medical treatment. Sometimes, the temperature of the cell rose and fell suddenly. Sometimes the light dimmed and brightened. If I took a nap, they pumped water onto my face. They checked my cell dozens of times each day. The female jailers would burst in and tie my hands to the small window of the cell. They would search my few belongings, looking for something.

They tried repeatedly to prove to me that I suffered from a physiological disorder. They never succeeded. Sometimes a psychiatrist came to ask questions like, "What's your favourite colour? Do you like seeing blood? Did your parents love you? Did they hit you?" I understood these questions and realised their aim. What provoked me most was the polygraph. I answered most of the weird questions honestly, only to find out the device was calling me a liar.

One day, a journalist visited me to try and trick me and prove that I was a suicide bomber, not a martyr. He told me, "Wafa, I'm so sad. I've lost my girlfriend, and I'm thinking of killing myself. What should I do?" I answered him immediately, "Our religion prohibits taking one's life for such a reason, but I believe it allows it to those who have lost their homeland and seen children killed." It was an answer he did not expect.

During the three months of interrogation, I hadn't been allowed to take a shower, comb my hair, or change my clothes. Even when I needed to use the toilet, the female jailers refused to let me. This was very humiliating to me as a human being.

When those painful months ended, I was sent to Al-Sharon prison, where the female Palestinian prisoners are kept. I felt as if I was moving from the hell of earth to its paradise, although both were painful. I trembled as the female prisoners received me by chanting "Wafa, Wafa." They embraced me like their new sister. My first friend there was Amena Mona, who taught me a lot and shared so many experiences with me that I will remember her kindness for the rest of my life. She taught me how to read and write Hebrew.

She was the first to teach me about prison life. One of the torture methods used against me was putting me with criminal female Israeli prisoners. They were fat and had no manners. They tried to distress me by going half-naked. When one of them asked for a cigarette and didn't get it, she tried to commit suicide by cutting her vein. They always stayed up until dawn, disco dancing and watching pornographic channels. I closed my eyes to relax but without ever taking a nap. If I had slept, they might have attempted to kill me. I actually heard two of them planning to strangle me with the TV cable. Had I not stood up and attacked one of them harshly, I might be dead now. For that, I was sent to solitary confinement.

While living with the criminal prisoners, I secretly got hold of a very short pencil. It was a valuable item, especially since our food dishes were covered with white paper. I drew on those papers and hid them. But a jailer found a picture I had drawn of Schalit on which I had written, "You will never see light before our brave prisoners do." These words and the drawing drove the prison service mad. They ordered the jailers to strike me and send me back to isolation at Al-Ramlih. They tied my hands and legs to the bed and hit and humiliated me.

Surprisingly, there was a cat. I didn't know how it got in, but it was with me in the cell. It was a companion to me. I used to hide it every time the female jailers came to my cell, until it gave birth to kittens. How joyful we were! But when they knew that those cats made me happy, they took them, killed them, and threw them in the garbage. That day, I cried grievously.

Nothing is more difficult for a girl than having her privacy violated, especially when one of the traitors pretends to be a religious man. As I sat in my solitary confinement, I was surprised to hear the voice of a man loudly reciting the Quran. His voice was so loud I thought he was in the same cell. Only a wall separated us.

Once he stopped reciting, he asked me, "Wafa, how are you?" After he uttered my name, I felt certain that he was a spy – one of those who are called 'birds'.

Then he said, "May Allah forgive those who sent you.

They were wrong to assign responsibilities to their sisters."

That made me sure he was a traitor. I didn't utter a single word until he was nearly hoarse from calling on me without a reply. I avoided that trap.

They also asked me to cooperate with them and take medication to heal my tortured body. No way!

I'm a daughter of Palestine. I came to be a martyr, and I have promised myself that I will leave as a fighter. So, go to hell, jailers!

Wafaa Albis with her family.

---

*   *Wafa Albis sought martyrdom by attempting to blow herself up in retaliation for the Israeli killing she had witnessed of two Palestinian children, Mohammed Aldurra and Iman Hijjo. Her diary reflects perhaps better than any of the others the tragic facts that violence breeds violence, and that, while it is possible to fight a just war, it is not possible to fight a war justly.*

Aloe And Its Peel

Na'el Albarghothi

33 YEARS were long enough to memorise all the scribbles on the wall. My memories mixed with my present and future. My eyes proudly observed a calm world despite the shifting realms outside. The conflict flourished, just as water pipes rejuvenates dry land, turning it into fresh green gardens.

A conflict went on between me and the jailer, who tried to prevent my brothers and me from getting anything, even oxygen. We fought lack with patience. We squeezed our hardship as if to extract some oil to lighten the darkness of our cell.

Forbidden fruit was sweet to us, but there was nothing to eat except some sardines, meat, and beans. We were often deprived of them, too.

One day the prison service surprised us. For the first time in 27 years, they allowed aloe in, although it was expensive. Prisoners distributed it among us, and they gave veteran prisoners what remained as a reward. I was one of the veterans.

When the one distributing the fruit came to me, he saw the wrinkles etched on my face, like the way water carves its way through the hard rock, telling a story of abiding patience.

I took the aloe with a fork, looked at it, and said: "Oh, I haven't seen this fruit for 27 years, though I have drunk from the cup of patience and resolution every day." Slowly, I cleaned the thorn with my hand. Prisoners looked at me, wondering, "What are you doing, Abu Alnoor*?"

I answered happily, "History should record that we ate aloe with its peel**. What then, my free people? Hasn't freedom come yet?"

Kounafa with salt

"The leader of the people is their servant." What a great saying that is! It resonated inside the prison, among its four walls, its chains and its hundreds of jailers. Among the inmates, Yahiya Elsinwar, Abu Ibrahim, was the most active. We spent our leisure time reciting the Quran, talking about politics and other things, and cooking as often as we could.

One day, Abu Ibrahim wanted to cook Nablusi kounafa, since there were many prisoners from Nablus. He collected some crumbs that we had, cooked them with canned butter, and added some white canned cheese.

I don't eat sweets or sugar. Abu Ibrahim brought me a piece, but I refused to take it. He insisted that I taste it. I told him, "I don't eat sweets, but if you want, you can cook kounafa with salt."

He looked at me and said, "Kounafa with salt, Abu Alnoor?"

I asked, "What do we have in prison, Abu Ibrahim? We forgot the taste of food and drink as we lost the joyfulness of freedom."

Abu Ibrahim made kounafa with salt. I ate it, telling myself, "How much I loathe you, my prison."

Farha, my mother

From within my cold, prison cell, I can't see when the sun rises or sets in the east and the west. I fight the cell and its grim face every night before recalling memories of my beloved mother. It is the coldness of my cell that wakes me at sunrise. It tries to provoke me.

It asks me, "Hey Na'el, how is your mum, Farha?" I answer it with tears in my eyes.

"Oh cell, could you bring me a house pigeon to tell me about my sick mother?" I hold the cell's bars and wonder, "Mother, will Allah give me long enough life so that I can see you again after this endless separation?"

My body has melted between the four walls of the prison, as my mother's has melted from sickness and separation, as if we were sand running through an hourglass. I am in prison, my mother is outside, and the Occupation stands as a barrier between us.

I have engraved your name in my mind, Mother. I imagine you smiling like the portrait of the Mona Lisa in the Louvre that I saw on the last page of one of the Hebrew newspapers I read in prison. I sing for you day and night with a broken voice, "My mother is a countrywoman who loves the light of the sun, bakes bread, has dreams, and cultivates Jerusalem in her children's hearts. House, pillars, fire, and alienation. Dress, song, sons, thirsty and hungry people."

When the window of the cell had been opened, I saw migrating Chukar birds. I asked them, "What is wrong with my mother? Has she weakened while waiting? Can you see another woman in my eyes?" The Chukar birds left, carrying no messages.

There is no pen or paper to write in the cell, and I do not know the language of birds to speak to them. At that moment, I felt that the wind coming from the west carried my longing directly to her window in Ramallah. She is praying to Allah to see me before she dies, saying, "Oh my Lord, protect him, for I have left him in your care."

My mother was the poetess of Kuobar village. She was strong and steadfast, one of the women who led the strikes and protests in solidarity with us, the prisoners in the Zionists' Occupation jails.

I saw her moving slowly towards me in her wheelchair, coming from an ambulance as my heart started throbbing and my head began to ache. How come the Occupation has allowed her to see me before she dies? She spent only a few minutes speaking the language of long yearning. Oh, how great is this woman who came to me as I was chained!

In 2005, my mum passed away. Yes, she passed away. Her last words were, "Say hello to Na'el. Take care of him. I wish I could see him before I die."

Once, I had a beloved friend, who was released with me under 'The Promise of the Free' agreement. His name is Taha Al-Shakhshir, Abul-Yassin. I knew his mother well. The smell of her cooking moved my heart. She was as kind to me as if I were her son. I remember her visiting and telling stories. Taha knew my mother as well as I knew his. He spent 20 years in prison, but we could rarely see each other. Years passed without us meeting.

We got sick of counting days, but I finally met him in prison. I embraced him and asked in the Nablusi accent, for he is from Nablus, "How is Al-Hajja (your mother) Abul-Yassin?" He nodded too much and spoke too little. "She died, Abu Al-Nour." That was a shock to me. I did not know what to say. Mercy be upon you, Um Taha. Moments of silence, waiting and sorrow passed as I tried to console him. Yes, Um Taha died in 2003.

Years later, I met Taha again. He asked me, "How is your mother, Al-Hajja Farha?" I answered with tears in my eyes, "Farha is with her God and your mother, Abul-Yassin."

After long years, beyond the limits of time, the curse of history, the violence of nature, and the brutality of the occupier, the right to freedom has been seized. This right to freedom is about more than having trousers to wear, being permitted to take a break, practicing sports for an hour a day, and receiving visits. It is about freedom from torture, interrogation and forgetfulness. It is beyond the jailer's imagination.

Allah kept His promise, and Taha and I got out. I spent 33 years in the Occupation jails, while Taha spent 21. Then I went to visit my mother's grave with Taha. I greeted her and others I had never met.

---

*   *Abu Alnoor means Father of Light*

**   *Aloe is a symbol of patience in Arabic. For Na'el Albarghothi, eating aloe with its peel is an expression of patience.*

Na'el Albarghothi was the longest serving Palestinian prisoner, incarcerated at the age of 21 for taking part in a commando operation that killed an Israeli soldier. He remained in jail for 33 years. He came to be known as Dean of Prisoners, but preferred to be called Abu Alnoor (Father of Light).

A month after his release at the age of 54, he married his childhood sweetheart, Eman Nafe, then aged 47.

Letter by Hassan Salama

Hasan Salama is a Palestinian detainee from Khanyounis. He was arrested by the Israeli occupation in Hebron in 1996, and given 46 life sentences (each life sentence is 99 years). He was in solitary confinement for 13 years.

Greetings and peace!

Dearly beloved, oh you who dwell in the great world that we hear of without seeing!

I dwell in a small world where I suffer the bitterness of isolation and detention. In this narrow place which daily grows narrower and narrower, how painfully we who are prisoners recall the images of times past – the most beautiful images that we hold in our hearts and minds.

How I yearn to return to those times, those times when we were still innocent and did not know hatred, those times when our respect for our elders was a sacred thing, sacred like a verse of the Quran. I still remember the days when we were on the way home from school, and there was a campaign to check the neatness of our books and notebooks, and I used to be the neatest. How I long to return to my home, my neighbourhood, and my city.

We miss those former days. Not only am I isolated, I am deprived of any friend from my region to talk to about Gaza or Khan Younis or about memories of childhood. I am growing old, my beard has turned to gray, but I live as if I were a child, yearning in vain and missing everything I love.

Dearly beloved, they want to erase my memory, remove me from the human world and leave me in the world of the dead. They want to leave us prisoners, after years of confinement, only with memories that are unrelated to humanity.

Letters are my only way of surviving. The only moments of happiness in this isolation are when I write or receive a letter from the world outside. I sit on my bed like a little child and cram myself into a corner to read a letter that has come from the world of the living, the world of human beings. The way I get it does not matter. The important thing is that I received it.

When I get a letter, I feel that I still belong to you, that I am still alive. I read every word, every letter, as if it were the elixir of life that brings me back from among the dead. This is what your letters, what your voices mean to me! I am desperate for ways to survive, to stay alive, to breathe. I swear to you, you are the oxygen I breathe. When I receive a letter I can breathe and live. Without it, I turn into a dead body among the dead, like a man in a horror movie. A walking body with no soul. For nine long years I have moved from one tomb to another. I stay in the tomb 23 hours a day, and am let out for an hour into a larger tomb.

But I am still strong, thank God, and I still have a strong will, although all the suffering I endure is aimed at breaking my will through modern psychological methods. I have friends here who were the most wonderful men, but they lost their reason and their condition became lamentable. Believe me, what I am in my strength and steadfastness is by the grace of God. God is the only one who stands with me.

Even you whom I love have concerns and problems that prevent you from keeping in touch with me – prevent you from sparing even a few moments from your time every week to write to me, however, a letter means life, the whole world and oxygen to me.

When you are bored, you can visit a childhood friend for a chat. What about those who are forced to talk to themselves and to live with memories that only leave them homesick? I grab my pen to talk to you and I find myself like a hungry and thirsty man who wants to talk about the thoughts of his heart. But my problem is that I do not allow myself to cry. I hold back my tears till they bleed into my heart.

I have begun to enjoy the way my heart bleeds. I feel that my heart's tears have sterilised my wounds and yet also increased my pain. Because I do not want to forget what my pain means, I do not want to forget my pain. I want it to boil like a volcano every day, so that I do not forget who I am, to whom I belong, and who my people are. I am still a human being and I am still alive!

How much time would it take you to talk for a little while every week or two, or to write me a letter and send it via my lawyer or by mail? By doing so, you would help and strengthen an isolated prisoner. I wish I could win your support for me and the other prisoners held here.

These words come from my pain in this time of tribulation.

To you who live in another world we have heard of but

do not inhabit I say: I wish you good fortune from the bottom of my heart and I will keep loving you even if you forget me so that my only comfort will be that I have God whose name is Al-Kareem (the Generous) who will never forget me.

Allah is very beautiful and I live according to His beauty every day of my life, despite my isolation, despite my anxiety, despite my captivity, despite my affliction.

Your brother
Hassan Salama
Al Ramlah Isolation (Ayalon)

Hassan Salama was moved from solitary confinement after the mass hunger strike prisoners staged in 2012. The lady in the photo is his fiancé freed prisoner Ghufran Zamil.

You can send messages to Hassan Salama via the International Committee of Red Cross by emailing his brother: akram.salama@hotmail.com.

Centre for Political & Development Studies (CPDS)

FOUNDED in January 2009 by a group of academics and experts in politics and culture, the Centre for Political & Development Studies (CPDS) is an independent, non-profit organization   dedicated to undertaking Political, Media, and Development & Policy studies.

The Centre is dedicated to Palestine-related political, scientific, social, economic, and development research. Its aim is to raise global awareness of the people of Palestine, their history and civilization, to foster study and research, and to encourage relevant cultural activities and creative youth initiatives.

Vision
To enrich Palestine through scientific research and creative ideas which support the Palestinian people and cause, by training cadres, spreading culture, and strengthening connections with other communities.

Mission
- To encourage scientific research in the fields of politics, development, culture, and humanities
- To train qualified researchers
- To spread a culture of tolerance and co-existence
- To strengthen connections with other cultures and communities

- To highlight the civilized face of Palestine and the Palestinians
- To introduce the Palestinian cause and struggle to new audiences

Goals

- To raise the awareness of Palestinians about national, political, social, and development issues
- To provide concerned Palestinian bodies with political- and development-related insights and recommendations
- To promote and defend the right of Palestinian citizens to freedom of opinion and expression
- To upgrade the vocational and cultural awareness of journalists and media professionals
- To prepare and train media and political cadres to play their role in public life
- To contribute to the preservation of social peace and the protection of human rights and Palestinian rights
- To develop the role of Palestinian women and youth in the community
- To contribute to the development of Palestinian society
- To promote and develop dialogue between civilizations, religions, and peoples

The CPDS has unbounded faith in Palestine's young people and believes that they have a crucially important role to play in raising awareness of the plight of the Palestinian prisoners and in fighting for justice.

The CPDS has organized several English language creative writing competitions dedicated to publicizing the abuse of the Palestinian prisoners' human rights to the largest audience possible.

The CPDS also holds talks, workshops and courses on how to invest in and mobilise Palestinian youth, especially those who have access to the outside world.

Yousef Aljamal, Omer Qaroot, Raed Qaddura, Dr Mahmoud Alhirthani and Akram Abu Anza at the Hashim Sani library at CPDS.

Photo Credits

We would like to thank the following for the photos and drawing used in this book.

Shahd Abusalama for the drawing on dedication page (page 5) http://palestinefrommyeyes.wordpress.com/author/shahdabusalama/

Addameer Prisoner Support & Human Rights Association for photos on pages: 10, 22, 26, 44, 60, 62, 77, 78, 80 & 96 www.addameer.org

Palestinian Information Centre for photos on pages 38

Centre for Political & Development Studies for photos on pages: 32, 59, 101, 117 & 120 and all the portrait photos of the prisoners at the start of each diary

AlAqsa voice radio for photos on pages 68

Ministry of Detainees' Affairs, Gaza for photos on pages: 43 & 46

Almasri Elyoom Newspaper for photo on page 64

www.bokra.net for photos on pages 76 & 116

www.psnews.ps for photo on page 91

www.paldf.net for photo on page 95

Muhsin Kilby for photo on page 98 © copyright

Al-Quds News Network: QNN for photo on page 110